HARD PRESS .NET

ISBN: 9781313272810

Published by:
HardPress Publishing
8345 NW 66TH ST #2561
MIAMI FL 33166-2626

Email: info@hardpress.net
Web: http://www.hardpress.net

CONVENT OF OUR LADY OF THE SACRED HEART, OAKLAND, CAL. 18..

J. M.

Silver Jubilee

Memorial

CONVENT OF

Our Lady of the Sacred Heart

Oakland, Cal.

1868 - 1893

1893
San Francisco Printing Company
411 Market Street

To Our Pupils

Always Loved,

Always Welcome,

Always Kindly Remembered;

We Dedicate This

Jubilee Memorial

1868 - 1893.

First Glimpse of California from
Steamer "Golden Age," 1868

Preface

✻

This little Memorial commends itself to the pupils of the Convent of Our Lady of the Sacred Heart in their moments of pleasant retrospection. Pursuing the paths and by-paths of years, culling here and there a flower of perfumed memory, it will lend a charm we trust, to their leisure hours, while it cannot fail to interest those who have seen their Alma Mater's young and vigorous life culminate in a grand Jubilee demonstration.

No event of the past is fraught with keener emotions or purer joys than a visit to the old homestead, dim as the dear old relic may appear in the twilight of receding years. So a ramble through our school days is attended with a corresponding degree of pleasure, blurred though our favorite pictures are, by the cares and anxieties of life, or by the shadows of time, which are lengthening and deepening.

But lo! a flash from memory's sun—and the whole scene is aglow—radiant with light, color and beauty. There are joys and sorrows, struggles and defeats, high aims and lofty endeavors—here, a wise counsel, which like a golden thread, has woven itself into our years. Now, a hallowed life, which has set its seal upon our own, again, an influence, whose power for good is abiding.

Friends outside the school circle, of whose names we are justly proud, have come into this memory banquet, and graced the board by their genial sympathy, their beauty of speech, and melody of song. We value the contribution, both for its intrinsic worth and for the gracious kindness which suggested it.

We leave you, therefore, dear pupils, in communion with this messenger of pleasant souvenirs, trusting to the generosity we have so well known in the past, that you will take it to your hearts in kindly approval, and still more kindly welcome.

Convent of Our Lady of the Sacred Heart, Oakland, Cal.
Feast of the Holy Name of Jesus, 1893.

Introduction

A. M. D. G.

On October 6, 1811 at St. Antoine on the river Chambly in Canada, a little girl was born to Sir Oliver Durocher. She was baptized the same day and called Eulalia. God had destined this child to be a vessel of election to carry His name and His holy truth to many. From early childhood she heard in the depths of her soul, the whisperings of the Holy Spirit urging her to consecrate herself to God's service. Faithful to grace and ever anxious to obey these promptings to higher things, she made repeated efforts to enter several different religious Sisterhoods ; but insuperable obstacles always arose to bar her entrance. These disappointments did not dishearten her, nor cool her ardent yearning for self immolation to God's glory. They served rather to increase that lofty aspiration to detach her heart from everything earthly and to purify its affections.

God's ways are always wise, though not always obvious to ordinary souls : but Eulalia Durocher was not an ordinary soul. All indeed seemed dark, yet like all great minds inspired by God to do great things for Him, she trusted and waited. She believed that the Holy Spirit who filled her heart with such noble desires would in His own time and own way show her how to accomplish them.

Having chosen for confessor the Rev. Father Telmont, an Oblate Father of Mary Immaculate, she opened her soul to him ; and under his enlightened direction, she at last learned God's designs toward her. She would indeed consecrate herself to God's service, but, it would be in a Congregation of which she would be the foundress.

The Oblate Fathers at Longueuil, were men full of zeal for souls and for the welfare of Holy Church. They gave Missions at this

11

time throughout Canada ; and in their extensive journeys they saw with much pain, the need of a superior teaching body for girls and young women. Many of the poor were very ignorant ; and the education given even to the richer classes was totally insufficient for the rising generation, living among a people either hostile to the Church or totally indifferent to the teachings of religion. These zealous men sought a remedy for this great evil by introducing from France, the Sisters of the Holy Names of Jesus and Mary. Negotiations to this end were opened with the Mother Superior in France ; but they came to nothing.

Father Telmont who had wished to send his penitent to that congregation, now felt inspired to organize herself and companions, Mélodie Dufresne and Henriette Céré, into a religious Community. He did so, and sent them to Longueuil, where Father Honorat was Superior of the Oblates ; and Father Honorat himself became the first Superior, and Father Allard, first Chaplain and Novice Master and teacher of the young Community.

Earnestly and faithfully Father Allard trained them to solid virtue and true perfection ; till having been transferred to Ottawa, and later consecrated Bishop, he was sent to Natal, in South Africa. He labored there till old age forced him to seek a rest. Providence called him to Rome, where he greatly aided his early penitents and novices whom he found seeking the approval of the Holy See for those very constitutions and rules in which he had so long instructed them. It was due to him that they were approved so soon.

It was on Nov. 1, 1843 that Eulalia Durocher, Mélodie Dufresne and Henriette Céré were formed into a religious Community by the permission and with the blessing of the Bishop of Montreal. After a year's instruction and probation, they pronounced their first vows, December 8, 1844 ; and in 1846, August 15th, they took perpetual vows. Eulalia Durocher became Sister Mary Rose; and when elected Superior, she was called Mother Mary Rose, the title by which we shall henceforth know her. Her companions were named respectively, Sister M. Agnes, and Sister M. Madeleine.

The new Congregation had a lowly beginning, like all great bodies that have done much for the honor of God. Its first years were passed amid trials, difficulties and great tribulations. These were years of poverty, of suffering and of heroic endurance in the face of strong opposition, sometimes even from those consecrated to the same cause. The Mother House at Longueuil was very small, one room serving for dormitory, study-hall, work-room and a place of recreation; another was used now as refectory and again as parlor. The chapel was 11 x 12 feet ; and its sole ornaments were a crucifix and a statue of the Blessed Virgin. In this house the Sisters kept, besides the infant community, seventeen boarders ; and so low were their finances, that in order to give the children enough to eat, the Sisters would deny themselves not only every luxury, but often the most ordinary food, their meals being often only *potatoes and salt.*

These privations were a source of real joy to the three brave women. Was not this the cross stamping their work? And must not the Cross mark all of God's great works? They were children of faith ; and they saw in these effects of poverty a sign of His love who chose to be born in a manger. Mother Rose knowing how God's children are purified and sanctified by sufferings, rejoiced in the depths of her great heart ; and throughout all these tribulations, she remained calm and happy. She looked beyond the breakers into the great future, and in strong hopeful words of prophecy spoke of the final success, spread and triumph of her children.

Not the least of the early trials of the Sisters was the death of Mother Rose, five years after her vows ; yet in that short time she had so imparted her spirit to her saintly companions and daughters that the Congregation scarcely felt her loss. She continued to live in Mother Agnes, Mother Madeleine, Mother Veronica and Mother Teresa. They had her strong faith and burning zeal for God's glory and the good of Holy Church. Very humble and mortified, totally forgetful of self, inflamed with ardent love of Jesus, whom they received almost daily in holy Communion, these noble souls carried on the work of their Mother. No sacrifice was too great, no labor too difficult when there was question of God's glory, and the salvation of souls. Nothing disheartened, nothing appalled them in their efforts to give a Christian education to those for whom Christ had died. Their hearts like that of Mother Rose went out to the little children of the land.

A three-fold blessing fell upon this rising Congregation. The first was its early poverty and consequent sufferings ; the second the union of mind and heart between the Foundress and her first companions who continued her work in the same spirit of faith and by the same lofty means ; the third, in the enlightened and zealous Spiritual Fathers whom God sent them ; viz : the saintly Bishop Allard, its first Novice Master and life-long friend ; Rt. Rev. Dr. Guigues, Bishop of Ottawa, whose devoted friendship and assistance it long enjoyed; and finally the venerable Archbishop Bourget, who during forty-two years was its father and constant protector. From the day he blessed the beginning of the Congregation in 1843 till his death in 1885, this great and wise prelate watched over all its affairs, gave it advice, assistance, counsel and protection. He was, in fact, a second founder.

The constitutions and rules received from the Sisters of the Holy Names in France were modified under his supervision so as to meet the wants and fit the circumstances of a new people and a new world ; and out of respect to those Sisters the same beautiful name was retained for this young American Congregation.

These constitutions as adopted by Mother Rose's Sisters are a masterpiece of religious legislation, and they display great spiritual foresight and an intimate knowledge of the wants of the people as well as the dangers to be met in supplying those wants.

The end proposed to one entering the Congregation is the loftiest possible—God's greater glory and the salvation of souls ; and the means by which this divine end must be ever and untiringly sought, are at once most practical and truly wise, securing first the spiritual advancement and perfection of the religious, and yet urging her onward in procuring the salvation of others.

They provide for the formation of thorough Christian teachers—heroic women whose time, strength, talents, zeal are all constantly directed to the one grand object. Hence the greatest discretion and prudence is demanded in admitting postulants to the Congregation; and when admitted, very great care in training them to be ideal teachers, religious, learned, apt, zealous—imbued not only with the true science of the saints, this is a *sine qua non* qualification, but also thoroughly instructed in all branches of learning.

If any have tastes and talents for special branches of science or art, they are assisted and urged to cultivate them. A mistress of studies chosen for her talents, learning and experience instructs the young teachers, and supervises their studies and reading; and the rule imposes two hours of *daily study* upon all.

This constant attention to the education of the novices and their formation into intelligent and practical religious teachers, reveals the secret of that marvellous success which has followed the labors of these ladies all over the country. The first teachers in the Congregation were of very superior order and highly cultured in the sciences; and there have always been among them many gifted souls, eminent not only for virtue but also for their great knowledge and marked success in imparting their learning to children.

Mother Rose wished her daughters to strive to excel in all that goes to make a true teacher; but they must be eminent for their knowledge of the Christian Doctrine and possess tact and skill in imparting it to others. In her visitations she was wont to impress this upon the minds of all; and the children would say, " All she tells us is : ' Love God and learn your catechism.' "

The Sisters of the Holy Names must be not only learned, painstaking teachers, their rules require them to be Apostles : they must form their pupils into Christian women, into women of enlightened faith, of high principle, of angelic purity and true Christian charity : they will in the words of the rule, (chapter I, Art. II,) "*inspire children with hatred of vice, desire of virtue and with the fear and love of God :*" and lest the good seed sown so lovingly be destroyed or bring forth no fruit, the teachers must as far as possible watch with renewed care their pupils after they have left the school and gone forth amid the snares and dangers of the world.

Their rule bids them welcome these young souls seeking counsel or sympathy, and when possible to unite them into sodalities, to procure for them good reading and all healthful help and association that may assist to bring to perfection the seed sown in the class-room. They must in the words of the rule, " Assiduously foster the *growth* of virtue in the souls of their pupils more particularly of those who having left school are engaged in active life." (Chap. II, Sec. 3.)

Though the primary object of the Congregation was the Christian education of the children of the poor and middle classes, as is expressly stated in the constitutions; yet from the beginning, the Sisters have directed schools and academies for the higher studies suitable to young ladies, and in these Academies have been given courses in *Belles-lettres*, the sciences, music, etc., and those accomplishments usual to a finished female education.

In 1863 the saintly Pius IX praised the labors of the Sisters of the Holy Names ; on Sept. 4, 1877, the Congregation was formally approved by the Holy See, and the constitutions, rules, etc., were approved by a Brief of Pope Leo XIII, dated Dec. 22, 1886.

Space does not permit us to dwell longer upon these admirable constitutions, nor to speak of the wise form of government they embody. In reading them and above all in witnessing their application to the exigencies of the time, one discovers the over shadowing influence of those two master-minds, the gentle Bishop of Geneva, St. Francis de Sales, and the soldier of Loyola, St. Ignatius.

The early growth of the Congregation was slow and steady, yet

MOTHER MARY ROSE, FOUNDRESS

BIRTHPLACE OF MOTHER ROSE, SAINT ANTOINE

FOUNDATION HOUSE, LONGUEUIL, P. Q.

with an energy indicative of its American origin, it pushed at once into the front rank. Beside teaching bodies venerable by their long and successful labors in educating the young, and in its subsequent labors throughout the Dominion of Canada and the United States, it has held its place with honor. This is due, after God's blessing upon their work, to the enlightened labors and wise administration of many gifted women whom God called to serve His cause of Christian education in the humble serge of a Sister of the Holy Names.

The Mother House and Novitiate at Longueuil were transferred in 1860 to Hochelaga, now a part of the city of Montreal. This is the residence of the Mother General and her assistants, and the chief Convent of this " Pious Congregation " to use the words of the Papal brief of 1886.

Since Pius IX blessed their work in 1863, the increase and spread of the Congregation have been very rapid ; and now it has Convents and Schools throughout Canada and in many parts of the United States.

In Canada it has seventy-four Houses and directs thirty-two parochial schools, whilst in the United States there are seventeen Houses and twenty-eight parochial schools. The pupils attending their Academies and schools number no less than fifteen thousand, and there are nearly three hundred sodalities under their care and direction.

However useful and pleasant it would be to follow the spread of the Congregation and to tell of its great work and triumphs in the cause of education, the limits assigned me warn me to confine my few words to their labors in our own State : and from what we shall see accomplished here, we may form a fair judgment of their work in other spots favored by their presence.

Twenty-five years ago, on May 10, six Sisters of the Holy Names arrived in Oakland and took possession of a neat Convent building on Webster Street, and a few days later, they began teaching the classes in the parochial school at St. Mary's Church. Only one of that pioneer band remains in Oakland, viz.: Sister M. Celestine who now presides over the school in St. Frances de Sales' parish.

On May 31, the first pupil entered the boarding-school on Webster Street; and this little school of the Convent of our Lady of the Sacred Heart has grown to be one of the finest female educational institutions west of the Rocky Mountains. Besides the great Academy for young ladies, there is a large Novitiate and Convent, and each morning bands of teachers go forth to take charge of three large and flourishing parochial schools.

From this Community have been founded the Convent of the Holy Names in St. Joseph's parish, 10th Street, San Francisco, the Academy at Ramona in the South, and that at Spokane Falls in Washington. The six Sisters have increased to be one hundred and five; and in the interval seventeen have fallen at their posts. Nigh seventeen hundred children are daily under their instruction, whilst all over the State are vast numbers of exemplary Christian maidens and mothers formed by their teaching.

With much reason may the citizens of Oakland pride themselves on the stately Convent by the shore of Lake Merritt—a thing of beauty to the eyes of men, and a place of benediction in the sight of God. Twenty-five years ago this site was in the country, on one side was wild, brush-covered land that formed a cover for rabbit and quail; on the other the hunter was lured along a silent shore by flocks of duck and snipe, mud hens and rail.

When in 1865 Rev. Michael King, Assistant Pastor at St. Patrick's in San Francisco, was appointed Pastor of Oakland, the whole population of the city did not exceed three thousand souls; but the young Pastor with true foresight, divined the great future of the City of Oaks, and with characteristic prudence he at once began to prepare for that future. He wished to have the mothers of his parish, educated Christian women, wisely reflecting that if he could accomplish that, his work as pastor would redound to the glory of

God and to the spread of the Church. Happy that land whose mothers are truly Christian.

Whilst Assistant Pastor of St. Patrick's in San Francisco, Father King met Mother Teresa, Mother General of the Sisters of the Holy Names of Jesus and Mary. She was on her way to visit her Sisters in Oregon and had with her a number of Sisters going thither to teach. At the request of the late saintly Archbishop Alemany, he made arrangements with the Mother General for the foundation of a Convent of the Holy Names in San Francisco. The Mother General promised to send Sisters ; and they were appointed and prepared to come, but financial difficulties prevented His Grace from securing the ground for a Convent as he had wished, and hence their coming was postponed until a suitable place and buildings should be procured.

Father King, full of plans for his parish now bethought him of these Sisters awaiting the call of the Archbishop ; and he besought His Grace to waive his claim to them for San Francisco, and to allow them to go to Oakland. He pleaded so well that his petition was granted. The zealous Pastor at once took means to secure a lot suitable for a Convent and school buildings. This was not an easy task when money was wanting, and few shared his own ardent aspirations.

Father King had what was better than gold, a stout heart and a strong will with a great confidence in God, and trust in his own flock. Not a few perhaps thought him over sanguine. Why should such a small parish undertake such an extraordinary and expensive work ? Was not the Pastor asking too much ? Would not a more modest school do for many years to come ?

His Grace full of prudence wished him to buy a plot near the church ; but neither pecuniary difficulties, nor the prudent suggestions of the Archbishop, nor the thousand other obstacles that arose could check the ardor or change the broad views of Father King.

He ever looked into the great future of Oakland : and he would build for that future. His choice of a site for the Convent was truly happy; and it would be difficult to have made a better one. The land having been secured, the Convent building must be erected. It was here that Father King revealed his true character and proved that he knew the hearts of his people.

Having procured picks, shovels and a wheel-barrow, and having secured the co-operation of one of his parishioners, Father King with his friend repaired to the land purchased. They took off their coats and having traced the ground plan for a building 30 x 40, began to dig the foundations of the first Convent of the Sisters of the Holy Names in California. The writer thinks a picture telling the story of this first day's work should adorn the Convent walls.

When the Catholics saw their Pastor pick in hand digging away like a common workman, their hearts were stirred and their better nature moved. Father King's Convent was not long building. His flock, charmed and completely won by his self devotion, soon put into his hands four thousand five hundred dollars; and by May 1868 he had the building ready to receive Sister M. Salome and her five companions, the pioneer colony.

Every year since has witnessed the increase of that little colony, and widened the circle of their work. Pupils have come in numbers to enjoy the great advantages of their teaching; and God has sent into their ranks many zealous, talented women, eager to serve God and instruct God's little ones under the banner of the Holy Names of Jesus and Mary.

This increase in number enabled them to open other Convents and schools. Hence in August, 1871, as Father King in 1865 foretold Archbishop Alemany, a colony went from Oakland to take possession of the Convent in St. Joseph's parish on 10th Street, San Francisco. Nine years later St. Lawrence parochial school, Temescal, fell under their care; and on October 5, 1886, Sisters of the Holy Names were seen teaching in St. Rose's parochial school, San Francisco. On July 15, 1887, we find them in charge of the parochial school of St. Francis de Sales parish, Oakland. But the most important foundation was that of a Convent at Ramona, Los Angeles County. The buildings were erected in 1889, and the Academy opened to pupils in 1890. Besides this wonderful expansion we must not forget the little colony sent all the way to Spokane Falls, Washington, from Oakland.

The little building erected by the zeal of Father King was soon so overcrowded that in 1873 a more commodious structure was built. This also proving inadequate for increasing wants, was so enlarged and repaired in 1885, as to make it one of the best appointed and most elegant Academies west of the Rocky Mountains. In this same year also was completed a large and beautiful Chapel.

The increase in the number of members has been so gratifying that in 1892 a large Novitiate building was added to the Convent buildings. We must also notice the purchase of a farm near Haywards, upon which is a pretty incipient villa, called Our Lady's Nook, a country retreat for the convalescent and the much worked and weary teachers. Hither they go on vacation days to find rest, and new vigor for the long hours in class-rooms.

The first Superior, Sr. M. Salome now in Key West, Florida, was succeeded in a few months by Mother M. J. Baptist who governed the Convent of our Lady of the Sacred Heart during nineteen years, with great ability and wonderful success. Mother Baptist was a remarkable woman of superior talents and great powers of administration. Full of the true spirit of her Pious Institute, zealous for God's glory and keenly alive to the importance of a true Catholic education, she threw her whole soul into the work given her Congregation. After God's blessing the great success of the Sisters of the Holy Names in California is due to the energy, good sense and tireless zeal of Mother M. J. Baptist. The happy results of her government in California pointed her out as a fit person to govern the whole Congregation; and in 1886 she was elected Mother General.

She was followed in the Superiorship of the Convent of our Lady of the Sacred Heart by Mother Michael of the Saints, until the appointment of the present Superior, Mother Elizabeth on June 22, 1888. This excellent lady continued the great work begun by Mother Baptist, in the same spirit and with the same happy results. To her motherly solicitude, her hard working teachers are indebted for Our Lady's Nook. Possessed of fine administrative ability, thorough knowledge of the wants of the country, and a great good heart, she is at once a wise Superior and a tender Mother.

With such Superiors who have been seconded by most devoted self-sacrificing Assistants and by teachers of great excellence, and by religious of rare virtue, the progress of the Congregation is no longer a marvel. The Novitiate is most flourishing and is a true nursery of saintly religious and earnest, enlightened teachers— teachers who have before them a great field.

The grand work done during the dead twenty-five full years is a pledge of yet greater work to be done. This Congregation has a great future before it in California ; the good done by the Convent on Lake Merritt and its zealous band of teachers will increase a hundred fold. It takes no prophet to say that Ramona yet struggling in the South will rival its mother in good deeds, and in turn become mother of many Houses and Schools. At *its* silver jubilee, the chronicler will record greater things than we have done.

Our introduction grows beyond its limits, yet one word more to point out a charming trait of these Sisters, a legacy from their gentle Mother Rose. She would have her daughters thorough teachers and zealous Apostles ; but before all they must be devoted friends and loving mothers to their pupils. Judging from the history of the Congregation, it seems to be a grace of their vocation to be such, and to win and hold the hearts of those who study any length of time under them.

This unselfish devotedness of these Sisters begets in their grateful children an attachment which is undying and which has a characteristic sincerity and strength that is as beautiful as it is rare. The writer has been so charmed by this devotedness in which there is no softness, and so struck by this unusual attachment that he deems it worthy of special mention, revealing as it does the work of the true Christian teacher.

We must close—The Congregation of the Holy Names of Jesus and Mary has deserved well of society and of God's Church in California. During a quarter of a century it has labored earnestly in sanctifying and lifting up thousands of children who have received from its devoted teachers a Christian education; and to-day they are training in California alone, seventeen hundred girls to Christian virtue, and instructing them in all branches of learning.

Happy, thrice happy that country which is blessed by such teachers! for they who form the Mothers of a nation, shape the destiny of that nation.

R. E. K., S. J.,
Santa Clara, Cal.

As we advance in life we look onward less and upward more. We say we are less joyous but we are more peaceful. When every outward object has failed us we turn to whatever temple we have erected within, and if the outside structure has not entirely hidden all, there will be bright star-flashes and glorious sunshine struggling down to us.—*Kate Kearney.*

For

The Silver Jubilee

of the

Sisters of the Holy Names of Jesus and Mary.

O Names of all blessing, O Names of delight,
The freshness of morning, the safety of night;
The rapture of angels, while seraphs aflame,
Grow fervid in beauty at thought of each Name

O Names of all holiness, Names of all power,
Before which the fallen archangels still cower,
And temptation's dread spells dissolve, like the ...
When the sun in its splendor the mountain-top ...

To-day, silver trumpets with gladness proclaim
The sweetness and charm of each life giving Name;
And we with the trumpets, exultingly sing
The triumphs of Mary, and Jesus our King!

Eliza Allen Starr.

CONVENT OF THE HOLY NAMES OF JESUS AND MARY
MOTHER HOUSE, HOCHELAGA, CANADA, P. Q.

A Wreath of Rhyme

(Woven for the Silver Jubilee of the Convent of Our Lady of the Sacred Heart, Oakland, California, and offered with fondest congratulations to the Sisters of the Holy Names, founders and faithful guardians of that Sacred Home of Religion and Science.)

Thus, from out the Sunset Land
   Love's celestial message came !
"Consecrated vestal band !
   "Bearers of My Saving Name,—
"Twined with hers, to whose blest care
   "Once her God His Childhood gave,—
"Rise ! and seek My Vineyard fair
   Waiting by the Western wave !"

Heeding well that summons sweet
   On the Master's quest to roam,
Left His handmaids lov'd retreat
   In their far Canadian home.
And, where Western hills are crowned
   With a fadeless purple glow
Fitting spot for toil they found,
   Five and twenty years ago !

By the quiet lake that hid
   Near a City's throbbing heart,
Shrined in calmness, well-nigh 'mid
   Tumult of that busy mart,

Builded they their simple home,
   And, Heav'nward, in the sunny glow,
Reared the cross that crowned its dome-
   Five and twenty years ago !

In the Master's service there
   Have they labored long and well ?
Let the ripened harvest fair,
   Let the laden vineyard tell !
Yes ! by countless treasures won,
   Favored hearts full gladly show
Fadeless fruit of toil begun
   Five and twenty years ago !

In the worldly desert air
   Blooming with celestial grace.
Or in cloister-gardens fair
   Finding safest, fittest place—
Winners of unfading fame,
   Grateful meed they well may owe
To the guides that hither came,—
   Five and twenty years ago !

Guardian of that glorious band !
   With thy vowed ones, now, to *thee*,
Daughters of that Golden Land,
   Dwellers by the Sunset Sea
First and fondest tribute pay
   For the love that bade thee go.—
Leading o'er that unknown way,—
   Five and twenty years ago !

Sower of the earliest seed
   In this Paradise-parterre !

Gather, now. thy labor's meed—
  Of its bloom and fruitage rare
Take thy guerdon. grandly won,—
  Grateful hearts, where ripened. glow
Harvests rich, *thy* toil begun
  Five and twenty years ago !

Fitting head of Order blest ! *
  When a *golden* gala-day
Shall replace. within the West
  Faded gleam of *silver* ray,
May'st thou greet its festal sheen,
  Saying, " Hail ! Memento-glow
" Of that blest foundation-scene
  " Of *fifty* glorious years ago ! "

Now, a fadeless wreath of fame
  Bring we, on *his* brow to place †
Who doth wear his royal name,
  With such meek and Christ-like grace,
And, who, at his Lord's behest
  Called ye, sacred band ! to sow
Heavenly seed within the West
  Five and twenty years ago !

Faithful shepherd ! Pastor true !
  Serving e'en His " least ones " needs !
Dauntless hand to *dare*, and *do*
  For the Master, hero-deeds !

Rev. Mother Baptist, for seventeen years Superior of the Convent, and now Mother-General of the Order.
†Rev. M. King, Pastor of the Church of the Immaculate Conception. Oakland.

'Mid his labors grandly wrought,
 This is crowned with brightest glow:
He these restal toilers brought,
 Five and twenty years ago !

And he planned their earliest home—
 Finding rest for Faith Divine,
With fair Science, 'neath its dome—
 And, unto its simple shrine
At his summons, came his Lord
 Living Manna to bestow,—
Love-sent laborers' rich reward,—
 Five and twenty years ago !

Now, a noble structure stands
 By the bright lake's peaceful breast—
But his Heavenward-lifted hands,
 And his Ministrations blest
Guides and guided still may claim,
 Still his care paternal know,
E'en as those who hither came
 Five and twenty years ago!

So, a festal garland fair
 His by sacred right should be—
He hath won a worthy share
 In this Silver jubilee—
And its star-like rays serene
 O'er *him* shed memento-glow
Of that blest foundation-scene
 Of five and twenty years ago !

Fadeless picture ! Still complete !
 All the band *then* gathered here

Twined in deathless union sweet,
  Brightly visioned, yet appear—
E'en the loved ones, gone before
  To the bliss ye all shall know,
Join the sacred scene once more
  Of five and twenty years ago.

Aye! enshrined in silv'ry light,
  Gazing from their home above
Sainted faces, pure and bright,
  Lavish smiles of fadeless love
On their Convent home adown,
  While each saith, in murmurs low,
" Sisters! toiling for the crown
  " By love promised, long ago,

" Patience! for a little space!
  Yours *our* rich reward shall be—
Passing feasts shall yield their place
  To immortal Jubilee.
Then, 'mid gleam of matchless rays
  Ye shall say : 'How faint the glow
Of our earthly festal days,
  Faded, endless years ago!' "

HARRIET M. SKIDMORE (MARIE

May, 1893.

'TIS THE capacity for sorrow that measures the refinement and
delicacy of the character.—*K. K.*

Twenty-five Years Ago

❈

Listen to the silvery chime of the Jubilee Bells! borne along the balmy air of May, to the violet-hued mountains of the Coast-Range. The great finger of the Dial of Time points to a quarter of a Century since the Convent of our Lady of the Sacred Heart, Oakland, first saw its Portals open and its joyous Pupils flock under its protecting spire.

As the rippling laugh of the scholars, old and new, re-echoes far and wide in the flower-decked rooms and in the perfumed grounds; let us reverently lift the misty veil of time and cast a look at the dear Pioneers of the beloved Sisterhood. What a fair vision meets our view.

It is the holy hour of Vespers in the Cathedral of the City of Mary, far-famed Montreal. The Bishop sits on his throne in the Sanctuary, surrounded by a halo of Priests and Acolytes. Loud peals the great Organ, and solemnly the deep-toned voices of the Choir chant the thrilling prayers of the King Prophet. The last sounds have died away along the arched vault. Innumerable tapers illumine the grand Altar; the incense clouds the air: the Bishop kneels in his Benediction Cope. But why, before ascending the steps, does he look up? We follow his gaze and behold, away off, above the Altar, six black-robed Nuns kneeling at the feet of the Queen of Heaven, in a small Oratory opening into the Church. With solemn prayer the Lord's Minister places them under the care of the Virgin, "Star of the Sea," for they are going to unfurl the banner of the Holy Names of Jesus and Mary in the far-away land of the Pacific Slope, and many a weary day they shall journey over the Oceans before they reach the Golden Gate of California. This is the eve of their departure, soon shall we see them on their way at the bidding of obedience. Gray dawns the early April day, but in the dim light we can see our dear young pioneers kneeling in the Chapel of their sweet Convent-Home, Hochelaga. Two Missionaries, bound for distant parts, are pronouncing their final vows; one, is now an inhabitant of beautiful, pine-clad Oregon, and the other, the leader of the little band, is dwelling in the shadow of the Palm-trees of the coral isle, Key-West. Not many hours has the day grown older, when on this 13th of April, 1868, the tread of many feet is heard in the hitherto silent corridor : 'Tis the numerous ranks of the Sisterhood, who have been warned by the sound of the bell, to come and bid Adieu to the six travellers taking their departure for the far West.

It is the 15th. The rain is flooding the streets, imparting a dismal look to everything around, but these brave pioneers wend their way to the dark, looming ship that is to bear them over the waters of the Atlantic. The deck of the *Ocean Queen* is damp and slippery, and the weeping skies have turned the azure hue of the Bay into inky blackness. But, lo! the dark clouds roll away, and the sun, darting his million shafts of light around, illuminates the scene. The whistle shrieks, the sails are hoisted, a thrill of life runs through the huge frame, the vessel has left its moorings and is turning her prow seaward. Handkerchiefs are waving sad Adieus. Our Pioneers have commenced their westward journey, they are straining their eyes to catch a last glimpse of the dear Mothers and Sisters who watch the receding ship. Let us follow them in spirit over the wide expanse and eagerly listen!

"The hours and days have come and passed like the foam of the crested wave. We are now at the 25th of changeable April. It is early morn and we sit on deck, looking at a far-away sail skirting the horizon. It would seem like a phantom ship, were it not converted by the brilliant day-light into a radiant object. What a sight meets our view as we turn our gaze westward : a long sandy shore, gleaming in the distance, tall trees balancing their rich, green foliage against the dazzling skies. The majestic *Ocean Queen* advances leisurely on the mirrored bosom of the great Atlantic and now, we see a small town nestling among orange-groves, and graceful cocoanut trees waving in the warm sunshine their plume-like branches. We are in the tropics. Aspinwall next greets us, the whole of the dark population turns out to see the anchoring of the crowded ship. To our northern eyes, their costume is all too scanty, but when we will have felt the overpowering heat a few hours, we will wonder at it no longer. We land with umbrellas over our heads, not that it is drizzling but the hot sun permeating everything, gives us too ardent a welcome. Now we are seated in the kindly shade of a veranda whence we can see the dusky people of the Isthmus doing their marketing. Look at the exuberant piles of the Golden-apple of the South, the luscious bananas hanging in serried ranks on the long stem, the delicious pine-apple with its crown of glory. The merry urchins run about, wearing head-gear made of the fibres of the cocoanut-tree, with green parrots perched on their shoulders, trying to sell them to the passengers going to California. Some of the foreigners buy the prattlers to make a new addition to the crew. There is a goodly noise of screaming, talking, parrot and monkey chattering, and guitar-twanging. At last we hear above all that hubbub, the sharp whistle of the locomotive. In haste we board the train and are carried across the isthmus at thundering speed, whirling past dark, luxuriant forests, with immense palm-trees waving languidly in the sultry air their huge branches of leaves, interlaced with long trailing vines, covered with large scarlet blossoms. We rush over the Chagres river, a beautiful little stream of limpid water coming down from these deep tropical shadows, to sparkle in

REV. MICHAEL KING
RECTOR CHURCH OF THE IMMACULATE CONCEPTION, OAKLAND, CAL.

the clear day-light. On its banks there is a small village whose houses look quite airy, being built on long stakes that makes the whole under part a kind of veranda, where the sleepy inhabitants may rest at leisure. Some of them look up now and seem surprised at the great amount of useless activity we display.

From the terminus on the shores of the Pacific, we are conveyed in small boats to the *Golden Age.* Our frail barks dance on the waters and tumble down the foamy waves like mere shells; it is rather uncomfortable, but we soon reach our steamer and are taken aboard. In the distance the quaint old city of Panama is lost in the glory of the dying day. The *Golden Age* has managed to secure 1300 inmates for the trip to the Western Emporium.

April is waning and we are still on the billowy home of the mariner. Our patiently plodding steamer is taking a short rest. We are on the Mexican Coast, right in front of Acapulco, and can hear the chime of silvery-toned Spanish bells. It is the hour of prayer in the old Church on that high white bluff running down to the sea. We seem to be locked in, as all around are mountains at whose base we see plantations of strange looking trees; their tall naked trunks would be ugly were it not for their glorious tufted heads. The town is small but possesses an old fort, which frowns on us, as if to ask our errand in this "terra caliente" of old Mexico.

The smiling month of May has dawned for us on the great Ocean. The Pacific has borne its name well for us; its waters ripple like that of a beautiful lake in a secluded dell. It is already the sixth, in the evening, and we are silently watching the sunset gates swinging on their golden hinges. Violet, pink, and soft sea-green tints spread over the heavens, while gorgeous clouds of trailing light fling the loveliest hues over the tranquil waters. Our ship is followed by the diaphanous colors and its huge blackness disappears in roseate beauty. By and by Twilight closes her eyes and the Queen of Night steps forth. Lo! it illumines the mountains of a distant shore. All breathless we look, and behold for the first time the dim outlines of our Promised Land, fair California.

It is May the tenth, we have, at last, reached the harbor of the great Metropolis that stands within the portals of the Golden Gate. Our steamer has stolen in silently, shrouded in the midnight gloom. What a glorious vision awaits our waking hour! A large city lies before us and though it is very early, the infant day having barely opened its eyes, there is even then great bustle and confusion. The street-cars are rumbling down to the wharf, carriages whirl past, busy men are banging baggage up and down, and heavy carts are already on their way toward lofty commercial houses. As we ride down the thoroughfares, everything is beautiful to our sea-wearied eyes: even the dust-covered shrubs by the way are an elysian verdure to us lone voyagers. Presently, winding up a hill we come to the door of the hospitable Sisters of Mercy, who receive us with open arms. Rev. Father M. King comes to meet and salute the little band that have traveled so far to help him in the arduous labors of his ministry. Never has the great heart of the Pastor failed us in need, and always has he been the Father and Guardian of his religious children.

We cross the bay on a little steamer and land at the " Point," a veritable forest of gnarled California oaks. Flowers are nodding their lovely blossoms everywhere and the air is perfumed with their fragrant breath. Our good Pastor's home is literally embowered in roses. Further on by the banks of a smiling lake, back of the lofty mountains on whose top still sparkle last winter's snows, in a verdant valley stands the modest little Convent which is to be our future home. We step down and the doors of the Convent of Our Lady of the Sacred Heart, Oakland, open to admit its first inmates: Sr. M. Salome, Sr. M. Anthony, Sr. M. Marceline, Sr. M. Celestine, Sr. M. Seraphine and Sr. M. Cyril. We exclaim with the Prophet: " Beautiful is thy tabernacle, O Israel! here shall we dwell to serve the Lord together."

A PIONEER.

Iress given to Rev. Father King on the Occasion of hi Feast Day, Sept. 29th, 1868

(AFTER THE OPENING OF THE CONVENT)

The year is clad in leafy garb
  Of crimson bright and mellow gold,
As if she mocked the angel death
  Whose stroke would lay her pale and cold.
Now fades the mountain's velvet robe,
  'Neath summer's warm and fervent kiss;
The warble of the woodland bird,
  We sadly in the valley miss.

The autumn winds e'er sing to all
A requiem beautiful and wild,
A whisper of the world of rest
Awaiting those who've nobly toiled.
Though freighted is its perfumed breath
  With sadness, yet a welcome day
Of sunshine does it usher in,
  Through misty shadows gone astray.

Our hearts all filled with love and joy—
  In gladness we have gather'd here.
To lift our voice in childish praise
  And love, to one, whom all revere.

But words are empty things at best;
　But echo feelings of the heart
And show unto a careless world,
　Of what we feel, the weaker part.

O Father, ne'er can we give thanks
　For holy work so well begun;
For purest training and the best,
　Of the persuasive tireless nun.
Within the sanctuary's pale;
　Within the chapel hushed and dim,
Commingled e'er will be thy name
　In our sincere thanksgiving hymn.

Forgotten, never, in our prayer,
　Where'er our footsteps chance to roam
Will be thy name, O Father, dear,
　Or our beloved Convent home.
And yet 'tis not an abbey old
　That has escaped the tyrant's grasp,
And guiltless are its virgin walls,
　Of withered ivy's loving clasp;

Nor old and mouldering column high,
　Nor ruined, crumbling, moss-topped arch,
In whispers low and mournful speak
　Of cruel Time's remorseless march.
A simple tombstone and a cross
　O'ershadows now the flowering sod,
And tells us that one angel more
　Now pleads for us in the courts of God.

Through infancy we look upon
　A vista of oncoming years,

And seek through dimness to descry
   The guerdon which their ending bears.
For thine own self, a monument,
   More grand than hero's laureled tomb,
Thou rearest crowning it with flowers
   More fair than valley's richest bloom.

But God, in justice can reward
   So holy and so high a deed;
The harvest may'st thou live to see
   Of what thou sowest now in seed.
To see this Convent stately rise
   Still guided by this Sister band;
Its pupils, may'st thou live to see,
   The gifted, noblest in the land.

When thee, the angel death will free,
   From weary care and crushing strife,
Oh! mayst thou greet thy children each,
   In that, the purer, better life.

                    S. M. I.

EVERY day is a syllable ; every month a word to make the sentence of a year.—*K. K.*

Remembrance of Sr. Gertrude of the Sacred Heart

→|·|←

'Tis the feast of the angel of healing,
  In the glow of October's late hours,
And the day has been vocal with wishes
  And wreathed with the fairest of flowers.

Like the songs and the smiles of the angel
  Of peace and of joy all the day,
From the true hearts of kindred and friendship
  What sunshine, has flooded my way.

What greetings and prayers, soulful treasures,
  That are part of the life whence they flow,
Tender tokens of selfless remembrance,
  Blooms too bright for this brief life below.

Blooms of kindness so sweet and so fragrant
  That they thrill me with grateful surprise,
For they bear on their exquisite petals,
  The breath of God's love from the skies.

'Tis the feast of the angel of healing,
  Of the angel of Peace and of Love,
But I miss in the glow of the sunset
  The gleam of a snowy-winged dove.

A message that never yet failed me
 With its burden of wishes and prayers,
But the sweet Angel-sister that sped it,
 Has passed from earth's pleasures and cares.

Still her mem'ry is bright as the crimson,
 That flushes the brow of the west,
And pure as the pearly haze mantling,
 The Coast Range's glorified breast.

O faithful Friend ! Daughter ! and Sister !
 In the glow of God's glory above,
I feel, that your hands are uplifted,
 For the Homes that here shared your heart's love.

For the Mother and sisters, that treasure
 Your memory as Love's fairest flower,
For the souls to whom Jesus and Mary,
 Are the glory and joy of each hour.

For the teachers and friends of your childhood,
 Whose prayers shall uprise with your song,
When the Jubilee bells of your Convent,
 Shall ring out their glad anthems ere long.

We shall beg God whose graces and goodness,
 Their calm quarter century have blest,
To crown with all joys His Heart's Spouses,
 In the city of Oaks, of the West.

S. A. R.
Notre Dame, San Jose, Cal.

Our Every Day Blessings

※

How strange is the human heart! so vast in its capacity for the grand and the beautiful, yet ofttimes so weak, so earthly in its longings and desires.

This little time-piece of our existence strikes off the hours one by one, and though they are fraught with numberless blessings, we let them glide on, in our restless eagerness to attain a happiness just beyond our grasp. Life is what we make it; and if we glance around us, how much cause for real joy do we not find in our every-day-blessings! Who has not felt the influence of a bright sunny morning; of the gentle breeze which having playfully stolen the fragrance from the flowers, has wafted it to us as though it knew its power of gratifying?

Who, while viewing the grand panorama of nature, with its gorgeous tints and sombre shadows, has thought for one instant how much there is to be thankful for in the gift of sight? And coming to the real living world of hearts that surround us, who can say, who can count all the blessings affection has bestowed? The smile of approval, the smile which encourages, are not these treasures of the soul? And little acts of kindness coming just at the moment we feel the need of sympathy and of love, do they count for naught? Ah! no; though trifling in themselves, they may be the pivot upon which our life's destiny turned, just as the sweet impress of a mother's lips upon the youthful brow of Benjamin West made him form the resolve of putting upon canvas the noble conceptions of his artistic genius.

MOST REV. P. W. RIORDAN
ARCHBISHOP OF SAN FRANCISCO

Gifts from the hand are silver and gold, but the heart gives that which neither silver nor gold can buy. Let us not then stand upon the ocean shore, straining our eyes to catch a glimpse of the ship that may never reach port, but let us manfully, joyfully board the skiff that lies anchored in the harbor, and though the voyage may seem longer, we will surely reach our destination in safety.

FLORENCE HYDE.

Convent of Our Lady of the Sacred Heart, Oakland, Cal.

A SMILE of approval may be a stepping stone to success. A look of encouragement from those we love may call into being slumbering resolutions and forgotten promises that will rise as so many barriers against our own weakness.—*K. K.*

On a Picture of St. Cecilia

IN THE MUSIC ROOM.

O picture in the golden frame,
  Fair as the morning sky !
Where is the charm that round thee breathes ?
  Where doth thy beauty lie ?

'Tis not the beam of light,
  'Tis not the lovely hair,
'Tis not the cheek of softest white
  That makes the face so fair.

'Tis not the smiling lips so pure
  That breathe with mute appeal,
Nor hands in childish fervor clasped,
  As if in prayer to steal.

'Tis not the mantle folded close
  Around the form of grace ;
'Tis not the colors soft and fair,
  Nor richly broider'd lace.

No—but the charm is hidden here
  In eyes of turquoise hue,
Whose pure and soulful depths reflect
  The tint of Heaven's own blue.

No passion could disturb a soul
  Lit by such flames divine,
Where hope and beauty, love and faith,
  In sweetness ever shine.

EMMA ROSENTHAL.

Convent of Our Lady of the Sacred Heart, Oakland, Cal.

The Priesthood

※

[Essay written February 27th, 1890 on the occasion of Rev. M. King's Silver Jubilee —25 years' pastorate in Oakland.]

The Priest! Before this sublime invention of God's love for man, the vaunted names of earthly grandeur fade into insignificance; the brightest lights of man's contrivance are but darkness in the Heaven-born rays of so mighty a sun. To announce to a world of ransomed souls the mandates of the Creator, to minister the rites of Holy Church, to offer to Heaven the sacrifice of Calvary—such are the duties of him to whose predecessors it was said, "Go, and teach all nations!"

The Priest cares for earth, only, as it holds the price of a Savior's blood; fame attracts him not, and glory cannot allure; for these are the rewards of men of the earth, earthly. Heaven alone has charms for God's annointed.

Wherever we turn, these faithful workers are employed; there is no page of history which does not bear the record of their deeds. Now, their voice is heard from the upraised pulpit 'neath the lofty arch of grand cathedrals; or. veiled round with floating clouds of fragrant incense, Christ's minister is offering before the altar the prayers of the worshipers. In the bustle and uproar of the mighty city, in the crowded tenement, where the victims of poverty are dying in squalid misery; in the far distant village, where privation waits upon the worker; in every circumstance, the same untiring guardians of the scattering flock are patiently sustaining the long and weary watch. On the blood-stained battle field, where shot and shell are menacing the lives of thousands; where the wounded and the dying are strewn thickest, and in the fiercest fury of the conflict, the gentle words of God and Heaven, spoken by the champions of the Cross, have soothed to rest the struggling heart of many a brave warrior.

No land is too remote for this Divine commissioner to proclaim the Master's words ; from frozen polar regions to torrid Africa and wild Australia, the same tireless toilers pursue their way. Savage hearts are subdued and brought under the influence of the Great Master whom they ignored, and their child-like faith, while it consoles the heart of the priest, often puts to blush the learned and enlightened of our great century.

Such is the royal Priesthood ! Such the selfless existence of its members ; yet, so unassumingly and silently are achieved these conquests, that the busy world scarce pauses to notice the results, until, one day, when long years have come and gone, all eyes are turned in wonderment to the golden harvest that the patient laborer has garnered in for heaven. Then, perchance, even strange hearts must needs join with those who have always been appreciative, loving and filial ; and, with one acclaim, lay at the pastor's feet their heartfelt congratulations.

MARY J. WORKMAN.

Convent of Our Lady of the Sacred Heart, Oakland, Cal.

Farewell

※

A moment, ere the day is done,
  I pause, dear friends, to say adieu,
To bid the past a sad farewell,
  To bid a welcome to the new.

What joy to 'scape from study's rule,
  And launch on Life's tempestuous sea,
To fly to scenes where wonders dwell,
  And, like an uncaged bird, be free !

Yet, ah ! my heart why throbbest thou,
  With feelings both of joy and woe ?
What means this mist that clouds my eyes ?
  These tears which now so sadly flow !

There is a sorrow in my joy,
  A sadness in my ev'ry smile,
As thoughts of old come stealing back
  And whisper, " Yet, a little while !"

I know the cloudless azure sky,
  Which hovered lightly o'er my past,
Will soon be changed to darker hues,
  Ere long the storms will o'er it cast !

Untried, I stand upon the shore,
　I fain would longer here abide,
I dread the ocean's stormy wave
　O'er which my fragile bark must glide.

'Tis ever thus—a few brief hours
　Of happiness undimmed by tears,
Our path with flowers now is strewn,
　With prickly thorns, in later years.

Since childhood my frail bark has been
　A fairy toy, on summer's sea,
With scarce an adverse breath of wind
　To trouble its tranquillity.

But now, 'tis gone—the past has fled,
　The future lies all veiled before !
I bid adieu to these old halls,
　To scenes I'll never enter more.

In later years, when Time's stern hand
　Has laid his traces on my brow,
I'll wander back on fancy's wing,
　To the loving friends I am leaving now.

Within a few fast fleeting weeks,
　These dear old halls will ring once more
With merry voices full of mirth,
　With stranger forms unknown before.

In after years, strange hearts will know
　The love and care which once was mine,
Then stranger brows will oft be decked
　With crowns like these, which round me twine.

'Tis sad to part when through me steal
    Sweet mem'ries of each treasured spot,
But sadder far, it is to think
    That soon my name will be forgot!

But though I may forgotten be
    When from these scenes I speed away,
Still in my heart there'll linger oft
    Fond mem'ries of this parting day.

And ere we part, with faltering lips,
    I thank you all, dear Sister band,
And you, dear friends, with whom I've trod
    The paths of school life hand in hand.

Dear Sisters, bless me with your prayers,
    Keep one lingering thought for me,
They'll waft sweet mem'ries o'er my soul,
    Consoling thoughts they'll always be.

ADELE F. KEYES,
E. DE M.,

Convent of Our Lady of the Sacred Heart, Oakland, Cal., June 28, 1872.

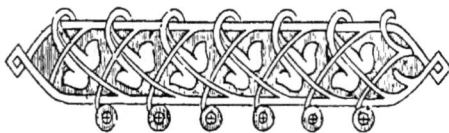

Mortality and Immortality

✳

The fairer the beauties of earth, the more perishable are they. Beauty is a flower of to-day, that to-morrow lies withered and sere upon the stalk.

In the early morning, just before Aurora draws the bolts of the Eastern gates, and Phœbus in all his glory mounts the distant hills, in that magic hour between darkness and daylight, what more beautiful than the crystal jewels that gem every leaf and bud? Fresh from heaven they seem to have fallen, to bathe the lovely flowers, before the sun has cleared the zenith, they will have vanished like a dream.

The fairest buds that bloom to-day in the gardens of earth, will have passed away to-morrow. What delight it is to gaze upon those fragile beauties of the field ; to breathe the sweet incense which they burn, their whole life long, in the temple of Nature. The hare-bell, swinging its turquoise censer to and fro in the wind ; the graceful pampas lifting its head in confident superiority; the immaculate lily, swaying its crested cup ; and the little blue violets nestling beneath their friendly emerald canopies, whisper sweet secrets to the passing breeze. To-morrow, we will find but a few withered flowers, and a sense of desolation will pervade the rural retreat. The amethyst petals no longer nod in the sunshine : the hare-bell droops as though weighed down by some new sorrow, and the lily's leaves are curled as though in scorn : the breath of decay has blighted the flowers, and naught of their beauty remains. Ah ! how sad it is

REV. THOMAS McSWEENEY
RECTOR ST. FRANCIS DE SALES, OAKLAND, CAL.

that mortality must thus limit our every joy ! Like the spectre at the feast, it ever stands, and with warning finger points, while repeating with the Psalmist : "And this too will pass away."

I have knelt at the twilight hour, when all was hushed in silent peace, and peered far into the purple distance where earth and sky meet in melted harmony; I have marveled at the beauties of the western sky, bathed in floods of mellow light; I have adored the Power that wrought these beauties, but ere I had drunk in one-half their grandeur, I felt chilled ; the night mists were falling around me, and darkness covered the vision of loveliness. Oh ! why could not that glorious vision last forever ? Why could not the artist who blended and commingled those aerial tints confer upon the picture the gift of Immortality ?

Man is free, he is superior to every other created being, he is master of the animal kingdom, and all its members are subservient to his will; and must he too, the noblest work of God, lie fettered in the slavery of mortality ?

Man too must die. But for him death is not the final limit of existence, death to him is but the threshold of eternity. For every other creature death marks the goal ; the race is run ; but man in this very point proclaims his superiority. The goal for him is also reached, but the victor, man, is crowned with immortal laurels, and the prize is eternal bliss.

The reign of death is not eternal. Immortality receives at last the sceptre and the crown, and reanimates the flowers felled by Death. The dewdrops that nestled this morning in the heart of the violets, gleamed in tints of rose and purple from the cortege of Phœbus, as he sank to rest in the distant ocean, and to-morrow they may begem some fairer blossom in another clime. They have not died : they have only passed from earth to heaven to be purified, and sparkle again as beautiful as yesterday.

And the flowers? Have they passed away forever? Will not the lily raise again its graceful head, and the violets nod a welcome to the passer-by? Aye, they only sleep, and will bloom again fairer than to-day. And man? He lies down upon the bier to rise amid angels and delight. The happiest hours of life are shadowed by the presence of Mortality, and the very thought, that transient are the joys that to-day delight the heart, is already a drop of bitter in the cup of sweet. The thought of Mortality is a source of annoyance to the merry, but it is a consolation to the sad. They know that death brings alleviation to every sorrow, and they welcome the grim guest. Welcome or not, however, he steals as silently as the darkness when "the day is done," and robs the dearest gems from the casket of love.

The soul of the great Socrates proved its nobility when it whispered to him that Death would only set it free. What material instincts inspired those philosophers who believed that the breath of God which He had infused into the clay, was nothing higher than the substantial form, and with it would return to dust !

Immortality is the great incentive to virtue. If we thought that Death is the terminus of life, how hard it would be for us to conquer evil and practice virtue. But with a soul, God gave us the instinctive longing after Him, and the knowledge that He would claim His own when our pilgrimage is over. Mortality should then be a cause of gratitude to us—gratitude that God has not placed us here on earth to toil and sorrow unrecompensed forever ; but has promised to share with us for all Eternity His Heavenly Kingdom, where tears are strangers, and Peace and Love are the wardens of the gates.

LUCILE EDWARDS.

Convent of Our Lady of the Sacred Heart, Oakland, Cal.

My Window

※

How many happy hours have I spent at my window, hours of rest in my joy, hours of peace and calm in my sorrow. Well may I love my window ; it has been a friend indeed to me. Oft in my bright, happy days of gladness, when life's waves of pleasure were surging all about me, have I sat by it, because I was weary of my fleeting joys, and longed for a little peace. Then my window presented to me earth's sights and sounds to soothe my troubled soul, and when affliction and woe pressed heavily upon my heart and earth's brightness seemed passing far, far, from me, then again, like a sweet consoler, it led my spirit, from the inward clouds of bitterness that wrapped it in their sombre folds, out into the sunlight and beauty that flooded earth and sky.

My window is the frame of those glorious pictures that are placed before my admiring eyes, and though the background to that painting remains the same, yet ever and anon, as the seasons come and go and day glides into night, Nature changes the color of the sky, paints the earth a different hue, places the golden ears of corn in the fields or blots these out, and strips the leaves from the trees showing me earth in all her wintry beauty.

Far off in the distance, the dark hills stand, and up their sides fair mansions rise, white and pure against the sky, each one just a little way nearer the summit. As the sun touches each one of these buildings, their whiteness is changed into a soft glimmering light, and as the windows glisten and flush beneath the touch of that royal king's hand, it seems as though the angels were carrying the bright records of men's good deeds unto the bosom of their God.

There is one hill that lies in a line with my window. Upon its side no stately mansions of stone or marble are erected, for there alone, lie those noble deserted temples of the breath of God, the silent, peaceful dead. I cannot look from my window, but I see that resting place, beautiful reminder to me, of where I some day shall lie when life's restless waves have surged from my feet away and have cast my soul from the sea-bed of Time unto the shores of Eternity. The cross that surmounts that hill, stands solitary and grand, alone in its beauty, above all other points of the scene seeming to touch the fair skies above, thus again uniting earth and heaven, as it did on that bitter day on Calvary's heights.

As I look through my window, my beautiful kaleidoscope, the fields lie at my feet with a streamlet in their lap, hiding itself in their embrace, like a beautiful boy in his mother's arms. The city stands further off; the sound of its strife and noise comes to me mingled with the tender babbling of the brook, subdued into a sweet, low, continuous murmur, and I think that if those sounds are sweetened to me at such a short distance from them, when earth's noise and clamor, its laughter and tears reach Heaven's gate, they must be softened into the faintest, gentlest refrain, pleasing even to angels' ears.

I have sat at my window at morn, when the grasses were still wet with the drops of water that Nature has spilt in mixing her colors over night and myriads of birds warbled and trilled the sweet tones of their melody. The fair stream went smiling on its way: I have gazed at my picture, watching Nature paint the sky a deeper blue, place a golden sun in the heavens, and then over all throw a veil of glorious sunshine, thus ever changing its coloring unto sunny noon and again unto golden eve, when all the glory of earth and sky seems to blend, in order to beautify the last moments of dying day. These moments are ever the loveliest portions of day's brief life. I remember one sunset of exquisite beauty.

It was summer and a soft haze filled the air like the incense that we scatter round our beloved dead ; a hush was on earth and all her creatures, for day was sinking, passing from time on the wings of night into the arms of eternity. The sun was resting on the dark hills like a king on his couch, sending his hand maidens, the glorious shafts of color and splendor, to bid farewell to the surrounding hills, and to kiss the valley and the stream good-night, while he, in all his royal beauty waited their return. Then the golden disk was seen sinking, sinking, until only a slender crescent remained, and that too vanished, but the sunset splendor remained.

The heavens were tinged with a soft, mellow, purple and golden light, while here and there a faint pink flush was on the sky. But over the spot where the cross marked the resting-place of those who sleep forevermore, the sky was a deep, beautiful red its luminous edges fringed with gold, a crown as it were suspended there, a mark of God's benediction. Then the beauty slowly faded, and night crept on with stealthy step, bearing in the dark folds of his mantle, the beautiful moon, whose loveliness he would reveal only when his sombre tapestry had been pinned securely down on earth. Then when he had pushed back his dark garment, the glorious moon, that fair sister of the sun, stepped forth and gazed with loving tenderness on the pale face of queenly earth. The lights of the city shone out one by one, like loops of stars let down from heaven to lead our thoughts, whence they came. So my window teaches me each day a new lesson of love and thanksgiving to Him, who has made all the beauty that floods the universe.

But too soon was my window darkened. They erected a building that shut out from me one by one, each loved object of my beautiful picture and with every blow of the workman's hammer, it seemed as if my heart-strings were being wrenched and torn, and my spirit crushed to earth, for the scenes that I love can never more be seen framed by the window that has been more than a friend to me : those paintings shall henceforth exist only in the gallery of my memory ; and now all that is left to my yearning gaze, is the sky above, and the cross that crowns the homes of the peaceful dead.

Thus it is in life. We stand in youth's bright morning, at the window of hope, and gaze on a world all fair to our young eyes and all that we see is beautiful, because our hearts are ready and willing to receive the beauty. Earth and sea and sky are flooded with splendor, the future wears a halo of glorious color on its brow, and we are too engaged in looking at earth to raise our souls to the heaven that lies beyond.

But soon the walls of sorrow and affliction, of age and blighted hopes, rise up before us and shut out earth's sights and sounds from our weary hearts, and when the future, which looked so bright becomes the present, its charm is gone and "like Dead Sea fruit it turns to ashes at our touch." As the wall rises higher and higher around our breaking hearts, nothing is left us to look up to, save the cross and heaven—meet emblems of our burden in life and our reward that goes beyond life even unto eternity.

CHRISTINE O'NEILL.

Convent of the Holy Names, San Francisco, Cal.

God only knows the stormy tumult of every life. His love it is that calms the agitations of the human heart ; His thought that spiritualizes the peace and joys of earth. He alone knows every mighty conquest, every ignoble thought spurned, every temptation bravely overcome, and it is He who makes Heaven the eternal abode of His loved ones, of those who have trod the paths of the lowly, who have sought the shelter of His love in their earthly pilgrimage.—*Kate Keaney.*

At the Shrine of Our Lady of Sorrows

❋

The slanting shadows slowly creep
Around this world of light and love,
They weave a carpet whereon sleep
The stars of evening's sunset hours.
The trembling rose leaves climb above
A lattice work of beauty rare,
Their fragile blossoms lightly sway
And shed sweet perfumes on the air.

The angel-lilies, fair and sweet,
A faithful vigil fondly keep,
As swinging to and fro they meet
And mix their fragrant incensed breath,
With breath of hidden violet.
The cool and palmy ferns uplift
Their tufted fronds of veined leaves
And fill, like sunshine, every rift.

Amidst these shades and balmy airs,
A refuge dear, well-loved by all,
Cross-crowned Our Lady's Shrine, appears.
O mystic hour, of twilight dim.

An added charm thou e'er dost bring.
To-night thou bidst me simply weave
A memory kept in many a heart,
A memory sad that does not grieve.

When first the rays of morning shine
And wake alike the flower and bird,
The ever pleasant task is mine,
To note the willing foot-step turned,
By groups of dancing children fair,
To pathway leading to this Shrine ;
The blue sky bending over all,
A benediction seems to fall.

At noon, the sultry rays of sun,
Well hid by leafy arch and bower,
Behold the quiet persuasive nun,
With humble mien and downcast eye,
Approach the cherished altar throne ;
Of loved duty 'tis a part
To lay each prayer at Mary's feet—
Her arms encircle Jesus' heart.

White-veiled, like group of angels clad,
The novice band serene doth stand ;
Their pure young souls forever glad,
Shine through each face with heavenly glow ;
No burdens on their hearts do lie,
For, casting all their cares on Him,
Who counts the bird on every limb—
Their souls in calm content e'er live.

GROTTO OF OUR LADY OF LOURDES
INTERIOR OF PIETA

SHRINE OF OUR LADY OF SORROW
ST. JOSEPH'S SHRINE

And, thus succeeding, one by one,
Come spirits joyous, spirits glad ;
Some, souls devout, at set of sun,
To lay their prayerful wishes down :
And some, to ask the precious boon
That innocence may ever know,
The soul that now is stainless pure,
Rivaling in its white the snow.

O, Mother dear, Thy sorrow deep,
Is marked by eyes that ever seek
To fathom mysteries that sleep
Beneath the closed lids of Him,
Who loved the world too well, too well ;
To-night, I ask a gift of Thee,
To live, so filled with pain, for love
Of thee, that all my life may be
A ministry to thy dear Son.

AGATHA SCRIMZEOUR.

Convent of Our Lady of the Sacred Heart, Oakland, Cal.

NATURE'S palette is the earth ; her brush, God's love of the beautiful.—*K. K.*

5

Not for Myself Alone

"Not for myself alone"
"O man, forget not thou, earth's honored priest,
"In earth's great chorus to sustain thy part."

Flower and beast and all created things proclaim the lesson,—
the noblest lesson that man can learn—to live not alone for one's
self, but for the world—for the elevation of the human race—for
the glory of the Creator.

Not for itself did God create the brook, sparkling and laughing,
now in the sunshine, now in the shadow. It must bring fertility to
the land, to help the pretty flowers and waving trees to beautify
the earth : and the flowers, in turn, must shed their perfume on
the air, and the trees must spread their branches and give shelter
from the noon-day sun and homes to the little songsters that dwell
within their leafy homes.

Not for itself does the ever restless ocean roll and break upon
the eternal shore:—deep, dark, unfathomable. It frowns upon the
pigmy man who has dared to find a path across its trackless main ;
nay, even old ocean holds within its unyielding palm the treasures
of the deep, and the treasures of the sky, and these latter he
yields to the ardent sun whose burning kiss upon his brow pleads
for man, whom all creation honors.

O man ! thine is the noblest part of all! Thou art the king
and ruler of the earth—" its tongue, its sword, its life, its pulse, its
heart "—forget not that thou must sustain thy part.

O wonderful race that since the day when Adam, fresh and
beautiful, a divine emanation from the hand of God, gave to each

58

created thing its name and part—since he stood, lord of all, within the Paradise of Eden—since he forfeited his birthright and passed out beneath the flaming sword of the wrathful angel, even to this day, when the world is transformed by his genius and all nations are as one—still is he king—still the ruler, glorious, compound, Godlike, and yet so human. So human that often he forgets his distant Home—so human that error sometimes smothers all remembrance of it, even all belief. Absorbed with the gain and riches of the world, life slips away, and heaven, God, and all his teachings are ignored, forgotten! And sweetest, truest of those teachings is this: "Thou shalt love the Lord thy God, and thy neighbor as thyself." These words embody the whole sublime doctrine of self-sacrifice.

Give, that another's life may be sweeter; work, that someone else may be happier; smile, and crush thy sorrow, that others may not be saddened at thy pain—Oh! they are countless, these many ways of self-forgetfulness; as countless, as the opportunities to practice them are frequent. And difficult as they may seem, and often are, what were life without them? It is the constant unselfish sacrifices that are demanded of the mother and are so willingly given, that shed their halo round her name in after life, prevent so much of evil, achieve so much of good. It is only self-forgetfulness that makes home-life sweet and happy. It is only that which makes a character great, a hero famous. And love itself were not love, did not the heart prompt self-forgetfulness and devotion to something ideal, and revel in the very losing of itself. And the greater, the higher the object, the nobler and more heroic the sacrifice must be, until life itself is given and man can give no more—as life and love are given daily to God in the cloister; as they were given in ages past at the stake or by the sword, or in whatever way and at whatever time Love demanded the sacrifice.

NELLIE COUGHLIN.

Convent of Our Lady of the Sacred Heart, Oakland, Cal.

"Dearest Lord, make us remember, when the world seems cold
and dreary, and we know not where to turn for comfort, that there
is always one spot bright and cheerful—the Sanctuary."

Fr. Augustine

Jesus dear, make us remember,
    When through life we weep and moan,
We've one Treasure, ours forever,
    One dear Heart that's all our own.

When the world seems cold and dreary,
    When we see friends turn away,
And the dear ones who were with us
    We no longer have to-day,

Make us think of Thee, oh Jesus,
    From thy glad bright home above,
Ready to send strength and courage,
    Anxious to give love for love.

Grant us when the battle wages,
    Fiercer and more fierce through life
Grant us Lord, sweet resignation,
    Teach us patience in the strife.

Patience, through the hard, hard struggle,
    Patience till the crown is won ;
Teach us Lord our daily lesson,
    " Not my will, but Thine be done."

Laura J. Brenham.

Convent of the Holy Names, San Francisco, Cal.

CHAPEL.

CONVENT OF OUR LADY OF THE SACRED HEART, OAKLAND, CAL.

What Makes the Summer?

※

Is it the lark's sweet hymn
  That rings out full and clear,
Growing sweeter still and sweeter,
  As to heaven he draweth near?

Is it the nightingale's lone thrill,
  That cleaves the cooling air,
And tells of evening's darkened shades
  And God's protecting care?

Is it the gorgeous rose,
  With beauty rich and rare,
Shedding forth its sweet perfume,
  From a heart divinely fair?

Is it the lily so pure,
  Of which our Blessed Jesus said,
They toil not and they spin not,
  They claim no glowing red,

But theirs is so pure a beauty,
  Such loveliness portrayed,
That e'en Solomon in his glory
  Was not like these arrayed.

Is it the dark-eyed pansy,
　That greets us with saucy nod,
Or the haughty sunflower following
　The chariot of her god?

Is it the magnolia waving
　Her snowy chalice on high
That tells in fragrant whispers
　Of joyful summer nigh?

Yes, all these things tell us
　That the summer now is here.
But other things there are that render
　That summer doubly dear,

Hearken ! from over the meadow,
　Comes the murmuring hum of the bee,
As he busily gathers his honey
　From the clover-scented lea.

And list to the drone of the beetle
　And the crickets' chirp sing-song,
And the weird tale that Katy-did tells
　In a voice so clear and strong,

And see the lowly grasses
　That cover hill and dale,
Wrapping the bare brown meadows
　In a beauteous emerald veil.

And see the soft green leaflets,
　That cover our stately trees,
Think you, is there no beauty
　In humble things like these?

WHAT MAKES THE SUMMER?

They tend to make the season
  So fraught with joyous hours,
The cricket's song and the lowly grass.
  As well as birds and flowers.

Let us then learn the lesson
  Which these humble things have given,
That e'en little things are counted,
  In the registers of Heaven.

One little deed of kindness
  May withdraw a poisoned dart;
One word of tender sympathy
  May bind a broken heart.

Then let us cherish these trifles
  That we meet in daily life,
And strive to smooth the pathway
  Of our brothers in the strife.

For we are heirs to one great kingdom,
  Heirs of the self-same God.
Oh! let us follow the lowly path,
  The path that Jesus trod.

MAMIE McGANNEY.

Convent of Our Lady of the Sacred Heart, Oakland, Cal.

An Allegory

It was a bleak day in November. The chilling winds of Autumn sighed about the bare and leafless trees, and swept over the withered fields. Here and there a few yellow leaves might have been found adhering to the swaying branches, but the ruthless blast tore them from their shelter and whirled them out upon the frosty air.

In the desolate fields a rose-bush cowered in fear and trembling before the wind—once so beautiful, now bare and dismantled.

"Ah!" it sighed, "why did they take me from my home under the sunny skies where the birds carolled forth their melodies among my leaves, where the butterflies flitted to and fro around me, where cold and mist were things unknown! Why did they place me here in this dreary desert to lose my beauty, and be destroyed by the cruel blasts of a frigid land!"

And the winds moaned sadly about and tore the few remaining leaves from the defenceless tree.

The snows of winter came, and the rose-bush shrank from the mocking flakes, that seemed to dance in glee about its withered limbs. The fierce winds roared and shrieked about it, and snapped its few remaining branches off and flung them to the earth ; and the rose-bush slowly drooped beneath the many miseries which it bore.

God saw and pitied its feebleness ; one day, when its life was almost gone, a ray of sunshine, like a heaven-sent messenger, touched it and melted the pitiless snows ; the merciless winds died down ; the gentle zephyrs blew softly o'er the branches : the warm rains fell upon it ; one by one, the leaves again peeped out, and the birds came fluttering to the welcome shade.

The rose-bush, all its beauty restored, grew and blossomed in the sunshine of God's love.

NELLIE COUGHLIN.

Happiness

✳

Were We Born To Be Happy?

It is an undeniable fact that in human nature there is a deep-rooted and insatiable longing for happiness, and it is quite as undeniable that this craving would never have been placed in the human heart to be left forever unsatisfied.

Well nigh six thousand years have passed over the world since the day that witnessed its creation ; never once in all that lapse of time has man lived and striven for other ends than happiness. Naught else could satisfy his craving, naught fill the aching void within his bosom. He felt that God had made him for a life of bliss ; he realized that sin had frustrated the design ; and yet, even the dread sentence of suffering and toil that drove him from his Eden home could not repress the longing of his heart, nor daunt his efforts to attain the end. Surely it must have been a seed of God's sowing that could withstand that blighting sentence and sprout to life in an outcast's barren heart. Thus within each man's soul is a source of happiness. With this store of sunshine within us, and so much that is good and beautiful around us to elicit its cheering rays, can we doubt that we were destined to live in its presence ?

✳

Is True Happiness Lost To Earth?

Man was born free ; he might or might not accept the law of his Creator ; Eden was the place of his probation—beautiful as God chose to make it for the monarch who came to preside there. This

same monarch willed to deface the beauty thereof by a rebellious act ;
then should we be surprised if the darkness of Dante's "Inferno"
enshrouded it in a gloom irremediable? But God is a father, and a
forgiving one like all fathers ; He could leave his disobedient
child to work out his years of probation under a cloud as dark as
that which hung over the cross, when in despairing accents the
Crucified called out to His Father, "My God, my God, why hast
thou forsaken me?" But His heart is so tender that when His
justice urges Him to repel, His mercy forces Him to take the same
lawless creature to His heart of hearts. Consequently, He would
not banish all happiness from this life ; He has left glimpses of it
in everything that surrounds us. It shines out in nature, in religion,
in the domestic and social relations, upholding us and shortening
the hours of our exile.

Around the hearthstone man may mingle with the loved ones
of home ; there also, the sweet companionship of friends has power
to lull his spirit to repose ; even when no one is near to share with
him an hour of pleasure, his mind can revel in a bliss his very own,
and in the exercise of his intellect comes another solace for his
loneliness.

But there is still another and a greater happiness awaiting him,
to which all else is naught. 'Tis the restful happiness of a soul at
peace, of a duty well performed. When in his heart this consciousness is present, all the burden of earth's anguish disappears, for,
in his inmost soul reigns a happiness supreme. All these pleasures
brighten his darkest moments and encourage him to persevere until
the day when he will be greeted with the words : " Well done, thou
good and faithful servant."

※

What Is True Happiness ?

As we stand at the portal of life's realities, we needs must pause
one moment on the threshold of the future and choose among its
offerings that which will make our life most happy. Some of those

who have gone before us have chosen wealth, some, fame, some, pleasure and gay hours of careless mirth ; who can say that their expectations have been fulfilled ? The history of the world proves the opposite.

Our soul was never made for earth; it can not rest in this stifling atmosphere : earth's gifts and pleasures are but means that aid to its eternal end. Whatever raises up the soul to heaven, whatever makes it more beloved by God, will be means of happiness here below, for God is ever willing to bless His faithful ones and give them a foretaste of the joy that is waiting for them beyond. We must ever do the Master's will if we wish to live in the sunshine of happiness : only the dark shadows of sin and wasted hours can make all around us black and foreboding and change the face of beauty into one of misery and despair.

Yet how soon our cherished plans are thwarted, how soon our hopes are crushed by misfortune or death ! Not so, when we are striving for a heavenly end. Misfortune cannot dim our happiness : each new trial, in raising us nearer heaven brings us also nearer to its joys : every sorrow, howsoever bitter, has its balm ; every cross, howsoever heavy, has its crown of light. Death, too, is but the portal of glory, and not the end of all earth's pleasure. We need not fear its chill embrace, for soon our Father's loving smile will welcome us home forever, and we will know in its perfection the happiness of which we have had but a foretaste here upon earth.

※

Does True Happiness Exist ?

Let me answer this by another question : Can an exile ever be truly happy while he remains far from his native land ? Does the little songster of the forest trill his merry notes when imprisoned in a cage ? Man's life on earth is an exile's lot ; he is the wayworn stranger in a foreign land. Even the wayside inn which he calls a home, gives shelter only for the night of life : when morning dawns he must hasten onward to the great end of his journey. The loved companions of his wanderings ofttimes leave his side and, hurrying onward into the rest from toil, reach the golden portals of home long before him.

We are ever longing for our native land ; and, when a ray of happiness falls across our path, it is but a reminder of the home towards which we are journeying, for no earthly joy can satisfy the cravings of our hearts.

The very nature of earthly happiness is a deathblow to the possibility of its completeness, for, unless moderated it tends rather to oppress. Again, what man is there who, in his happiest hours, has not felt an indescribable dread of the loss thereof, a presentiment that even while he drinks, the cup will be dashed from his eager lips ? Yes, on every page of life's history is written with tears of sorrow the sad tale of disappointed happiness. On the very first page, we find the dead leaves of Eden's fairest flowers.

Life is one continual awakening from momentary bliss to real sorrow; many a face wears a happy look while deep down in the heart is a grave, where lies some cherished hope, or some bright dream long since laid away. All our joys walk in sorrow's shadow ; tears and laughter follow close upon each other. " O man, thou pendulum 'twixt a smile and a tear ! "

But as though to urge us on and to encourage us on the long weary path, it seems for a moment as though the Eternal Gates stood ajar and we catch a glimmer of the glory that falls to us from that radiant Home. We then experience a peace and happiness that our weak human nature must call perfect ; although its gold is mingled, alas ! with the dross of earth. Encouraged by the beauteous vision, we go on, braver and better for the foretaste of the blessings beyond. Earthly felicity is to unalloyed happiness, what the blossom is to the fruit—only a promise, for man's inheritance on earth is sorrow. Having this, he will not cease to strive and long for that true Home where Mercy's hand shall brush away every tear, and happiness unclouded will be his forever.

Why Is There So Little Happiness?

The beautiful vision called happiness assumes many a form and semblance, according to the ideal that is formed by those who seek it. Sometimes it is a picture of earthly triumph and world-wide fame that lures man on to deeds of grandeur and bravery; sometimes the phantom is of beauteous mien; richest robes bedecked with jewels, clothe the graceful form, the dainty hand beckons the deluded victim, and untrammeled pleasure claims another follower.

But is not this a happy lot to follow, to overtake such dreams of loveliness? Yes, it would be bliss indeed, if attainment could satisfy all expectation. But it is not so. No sooner does the admiration of a world rise up before the conqueror, than the sickening void within his bosom seems to echo the myriad voices that proclaim how vain and empty is the glory that once shone so resplendent.

The very consciousness that the long-sought joy is in his grasp makes the beauty that once enticed the youthful mind, a source of anguish to the fortunate possessor; he now realizes that it was only distance that made the scene enchanting. The lovely phantom of wealth, fame, and pleasure never is overtaken, for when we reach the spot where, but an instant before, she stood, we find that she has fled.

Thus all life long the chase is followed in vain, because we search for happiness where it is not, like one who in the dark goes round and round his destination, never dreaming it lies so near, thinking to find happiness in riches, or in worldly honors, while it lies quietly by his side in his daily avocations. Nor will he search in sorrow's cup for the magic gift, but fly with frightened heart from every shadow of suffering, forgetting that Gethsemane and Calvary lay on the road to Olivet, and that God is often pleased to place the most ennobling happiness at the bottom of a deep draught of sorrow.

Ah ! if we could view life's winding vale from death's dark mount, there we would see where each deceptive pathway leads, and choose that which takes us straight to God.

※

Which Are Our Happiest Days ?

In every life record we find days blotted and blurred with tears ; but not according to these must we judge of the individual's life, but rather according to those catalogued as red-letter days. A red-letter day, or one of special and striking happiness, is not merely a day of gay festivities or a succession of pleasurable emotions. Such a day may be nothing more than a kind of torpor, all desires and restless craving for something higher and more lasting having been lulled to rest by intoxicating excitement and sheer animal enjoyment, thus producing a temporary counterfeit of bliss.

Which then are our happiest days? Are they the "days of triumph and of mirth"? The days when scenes of earth's fair beauty crowd around? The days when admiration wafts sweet incense to the hero of the hour? No, far from it. They are days of stillness and repose, when, unnoticed by the surging throng, some deed of worth in God's pure sight is wrought in secret and alone. They are days when self is all forgotten ; days when a fellow-creature claims our best endeavor ; days in which we experience after a duty well done, that sweet calm which is the friend of a pure conscience, and which surpasses all that the world can offer.

Adulations add not to this joy supreme, for when most neglected, most despised, the heart may be happiest. A writer has beautifully said, "In vain do they talk of happiness, who never subdued an impulse in obedience to a principle. He who never sacrifices a present to a future good, or a personal to a general cause, can speak of happiness only as the blind do of colors."

The pathway of faithfulness is rugged, and every step calls forth a pang to compensate for every joy. But, oh! who can compare the sacrifice with the achievement, the anguish with the bliss?

※

THE BANE OF TRUE HAPPINESS

Cast a glance around you and see where happiness dwells not. In her place you will see selfishness sitting enthroned in the human heart and keeping happiness far off, while its victim wanders on, longing and searching for the magic gift. Men would enjoy happiness alone, and their jealous hearts forbid others to enjoy it with them. They do not see that she is not a creature of solitude, that she cannot abide in narrow hearts, but delights to dwell in the large and generous soul ; with strange inconsistency, she comes to us in all her charms, only when we are striving to hire her to visit a fellow-man.

The man who selfishly hoards his joys, and thinks to increase them, is like one who, looking at his own full granary, which he boasts of keeping from the soil and mill, marvels at his neighbors' wastefulness when they sow in the Spring. The golden Autumn comes, and while he has only his few bushels preserved, their fields are yellow with an abundant harvest.

Our peace and joy must flow out to others like "gifts and attainments which are not only destined to be light and warmth in our own dwellings, but are as well to shine through the window in the dark night, to guide and cheer bewildered travelers upon the road."

"Live not to thyself alone," but give of the little God has given thee ; then in the effort made to throw sunshine into the life of a brother, our own hearts will catch the light that is reflected, and we will be happy in the consciousness of making others happy.

Tennyson has said : " Dark is the world to thee; thyself art the reason why."

As we are each weaving our web of life, we can put bright colors on Time's loom, or we can weave our web all one dull dark gray. The task lies before us; the power and the means we have. Will each coming moment beam with happiness? It rests with us and is contained in one short word—*unselfishness*. If men were but unselfish, if the rich would look beyond the narrow horizon of their own bright clime to the wintry realm of the poor ; if each would give a helping hand to some weak brother, this earth would soon become all peace, all bliss, and naught but "good will" reign among the sons of men.

❋

WHAT SHALL I DO TO BE HAPPY ?

We sit in the darkness and gloom of selfishness and ask this piteous question with clouded face that portrays the want of true happiness within our souls.

Our Divine Master Himself was our teacher when He said, " Be thou faithful until death, and I will give thee the crown of eternal life." Faithfulness in accomplishing our duty will win for us eternal happiness ; and although God promises a full reward only after this life, yet every one has felt that even here the reward of sweet peace and content follows a duty well performed. Duty is not a meager accomplishment of our daily avocations, not the hard unsympathetic meting out of justice ; but it is our every action done with love.

Life for the most part is made up of little things : each thought, each act, lends its aid to make up the sum of a life-time. Few are called to glorious deeds, but all to do their best, however small it may be. An active life, full of kindness is always the happiest. One word of encouragement that cheers a fainting brother ; one word of brightness that brings a smile to some care-worn counte-nance ; one word of Heaven that raises up some soul from earth ; even a tender thought of pity that may not venture beyond the precincts of the heart—all these have power to make our lives most

ST. MARY'S SCHOOL, OAKLAND   ST. LAWRENCE SCHOOL, TEMESCAL

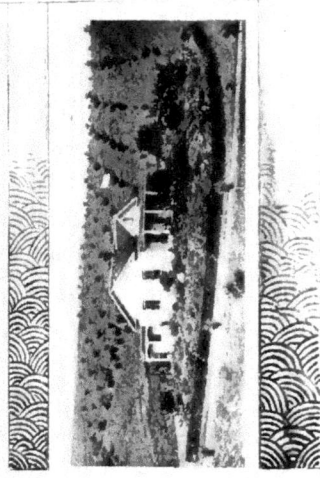

ST. FRANCIS DE SALES SCHOOL, OAKLAND   GLIMPSE OF OUR LADY'S NOOK

happy. And if these little things can bring happiness, how much more will it follow a prayer well said, a duty bravely done, a triumph over self—the hardest of life's battles !

With the impress of time we should grow more thoughtful, more generous, more self-sacrificing, and consequently more ready to bestow kindness upon our fellow-creatures. For we have learned by experience how often we stand in need of hearing what we know full well ; our own balsam must be poured into our hearts by another's hand.

Let us ever bear in mind that " Happiness is a perfume, and we cannot pour it upon others without getting a few drops ourselves."

※

No Virtue, No Happiness

Earth with all its pleasures and its beauties, was born to die ; man's doom was uttered in Eden. " Dust thou art and to dust thou shalt return." Man's soul alone can escape annihilation, for it was made for Heaven and immortality. It is now a prisoner chained to its cell by the very life that we endeavor to enjoy. If to earth we cling, with it we shall pass away. The tiny insect that loves to dwell in the frail cup of the wayside flow'ret will, when the dainty blossom fades, be trampled with it in the dust of the roadside.

All happiness is false that has not virtue as a foundation. Virtue alone can give that peace, that rest, and that bliss for which man has been created. Alas ! he has not always been consistent : he has wandered into by-paths ; he has sought after happiness in the accumulation of worldly goods, in the gratification of the sensual appetite. But he has sought in vain, until the soul, which is a breath of life from God's bosom, great, noble and expansive, has become little, narrow, and craving, after the " husks of swine in a far-off country," removed from God's grace and blessing, and consequently from true happiness.

How impossible for happiness and vice to dwell together ! As well might the dove and the tiger lie down together in sweet companionship. Happiness is heaven-born, vice sprang into being when the bright sun of Lucifer had set forever. How can all the beauties, all the pleasures of the world delight the man whose soul is hardened with sin ? He may gaze on the loveliness around, he may listen to the joyous strains of music, he may dwell in the midst of comfort and luxury ; yet ever within his bosom a voice will reproach. In every beauty there will lurk a mocking demon ; in every strain of music there will be an undertone of despair ; in all the pleasures of wealth, will lie in waiting some frightful vision to dash away his dreams of happiness.

Virtue is the handmaid of Happiness ; she goes before to prepare hearts for her reception. When all is ready, Happiness enters with that " peace which the world cannot give," and the heart rests secure in that joy " which no man shall take from it."

※

Earthly Happiness, a Reflection of Heaven

" We see now through a glass darkly ; but then, face to face." While all our life's best efforts are made for the sole great boon of happiness, the inmost soul ever breathes the same refrain, " Earth cannot know happiness." God has given these fleeting gleams of brightness to light our homeward path, and not to give us full enjoyment while still we linger in our dreary exile. He has placed around us loved ones, not that our hearts should look no further, but that in their virtues we should find reminders of the Infinite Loveliness beyond. How much better we will know and love them when we greet them in the Home above ! Then the untrammeled soul will reveal all those beauties we could not know fully before.

Life is a mighty work-room where the kind Master has hung, here and there, mirrors that give to the laborer's upturned eyes, passing reflections of the azure heavens. These pictures of beauty are unseen by those whose gaze is ever riveted below, and only those who look above in their hours of lowly labor can view the loveliness therein depicted. Then, too, their designs will be most beauteous, for they will work in scenes of purest beauty. And yet, look at the bent form of the laborers. How few raise their eyes above! How many are seeking models from the dusty floor! How many are regardless of the Master's kind endeavor for their success! Surely they can never hope to achieve their end ; for while they are wasting the precious moments in vain search for what they cannot find, the twilight is closing upon them and the Master comes to view the results of the day's labor. Confusion and shame are now their portion, and the shadows of night bring for them no peaceful home of joyful rest, but darkness and despair.

Oh ! let us ever raise our eyes to Heaven amid the toils of life. Then when twilight brings the close of day, all the labor of our life's hours will surely be blessed of God.

Class of '90

Edith ould
Blanche Belden
Dora Bryant
Mamie Cahill
Kate Fitzwilliam

Lucile Kesner
Mamie Lewis
Agnes C Abel
Mabel Watson
Mary Lockman

Convent of our Lady of the Sacred Heart, Oakland, Cal.

The Mission of the Snowflake

❊

A soft feathery snowflake drifted slowly down to earth, who extended her arms and folded the pale wanderer to her heart. "Lie here, little one," she whispered low, "lie here till my fair daughter Spring comes in her youthful beauty ; then shalt thou make choice of a state of existence from the many that I will show to thee." All through the winter the snowflake slumbered, till at last it heard in the distance the sweet carol of birds, and all the air seemed one vast storehouse of rare perfumes. Then it felt a wonderful restlessness steal over its spirit and said to Mother Earth : "Let me go forth ; give me some aim in life, for I can no longer abide this sleeping away of my time." "Thou art right, my child," she answered, "'Tis time to choose how thou wilt serve thy Maker. Many are the snowflakes that I have cherished in my heart and placed at length where God needed them most. See the vast Ocean: his waters like a silvery zone girdle me round ; his snow-capped waves are ever saluting me as they bear in chivalric pride rich treasures to my store—coral that rivals the red of fairest maidens' lips ; pearls that the haughtiest of my children stoop to gather ; while the shells and moss that he brings to me have tints and texture so delicate that man with all his boasted art can only admire—equal he cannot. He yields me constant incense in the vapors that are rising from his waters. These float over me and cool the winds that come sighing in the languishing summer time. Again they fall as gentle rain on the thirsty flowers. But ofttimes the flowers have not need for all that the grand and generous old ocean sends in the rain ; yet I do not permit it to waste, I treasure it up. Deep in my bosom it sinks, and bye and bye I show it some tiny opening where it trickles down through a rocky crevice. First, slowly and noiselessly it runs along, but as it finds its pathway growing wider, it laughs to itself with a rippling sound which the hills and woods around give back with a merrier echo, while the valley now lays off its garb of sombre brown, and dons a suit of richest green with royal trimmings of purple and gold. Deeper and wider the tiny stream grows, with a song ever on its lips as it plays around the stones that lie in its way, for now it knows it is drawing near to its ocean home. Nearer and nearer it draws, now it lays aside the careless air, as it thinks of its mighty origin—majesty and sublimity mark its closing path. The gurgling, splashing music, that accompanied the turning of the village mill-wheel, and the placid waters that mirror each sweet maid as she lingers on the rustic bridge to gaze with dreamy eyes into the brooklet's depths, now give way to the roar and dash of a Niagara's furious waters or the deep mysterious flow of a grand and mighty river. At length it reaches once more the mighty ocean who takes it into his arms and listens to the story of all its doings.

" I have other means of storing the beauty of the ocean. I seize the rain in its passage over my mountain heights, and I turn its diamonds into pearls ; then I form a cloth of these jewels and I spread it over my coldest regions to warm my children beneath ; and some of the moisture that ladens the air I gather in crystal drops to gem the delicate flowers. On the tall fair lily and the graceful bluebell I hang these jewels, and even seek out the modest violet hiding away under velvety hangings to deck it with my fairest gems. All this and much more do I owe to the ocean with its bountiful waters, but God has added another gift to please my children here, and give them the hopes of a brighter life when this has passed away. When the rain falls like my children's tears, God smiles a smile of comforting love and there comes in the skies a beautiful bow, penciled with sunbeams and dyed with many and glorious hues, and his children take comfort therefrom. Hope lives once more in their bosoms with strength renewed ; they take up once more life's burden which before they bore so wearily. Now little snowflake choose from these ; what shall thy mission be? And the snowflake softly answered, " Not in the dew would I live, for this passes away with the morning sun : nor in the stream, though happy its mission, but I would rise from lowly things—I would draw near to man's Maker. I would dwell in His beautiful bow that I might give to thy children, O Earth, hope in their hour of despair, and strength to carry the burden of life. But more, far more than this would I do, for I would teach them to love."

KATE FITZWILLIAM,
Convent of our Lady of the Sacred Heart, Oakland, Cal.

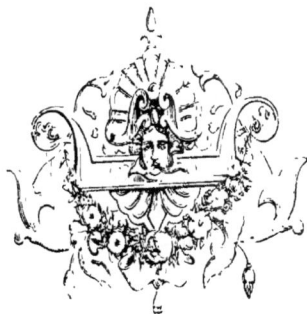

My Convent Home

How sweet the above words sound to our ears! But far sweeter is the blissful realization of their true meaning, for it is a home worthy of the name it bears. 'Tis a lovely spot encircled by a band of cypress trees, some of which rear their lofty heads toward the smiling heavens and stretch out their hospitable arms, seeming to invite us to rest beneath their shadows. Grand and majestic rises the stately building, like some enchanted castle, with its circling foliage of shady trees, velvet lawns, bright patches of smiling flowers, and inviting orchards with their wealth of golden fruit, made unapproachable by a green hedge over which sundry longing peeps are taken by curious school girls. Overlooking all is the cross-crowned tower, mounting proudly to the smiling skies. In the background, peering through green arches gleaming with its heaven-borrowed hues, is a quiet lake upon whose placid bosom countless white sails are continually flitting. On loved holidays the " Rosa," " Aloysius " and " Swan " go forth to swell the number of fairy crafts, each bearing a happy freight of laughing school-girls, whose merry voices float out upon the breeze as they skim over the waters of the blue lake.

Leaving the happy rowers to enjoy their boat ride, we will take a stroll through the grounds, and admire God's fairest gifts, the flowers, which he has so generously bestowed upon this one of His favorite spots. All are here, from the stately sun-flower to the modest violet that peers shyly up as we pass by. There is one spot carefully circled by faithful cypress, where white flowers bloom untouched by childish fingers, where the drooping willow keeps a tender watch over two lonely graves. The black cross, marking the resting place of one of God's chosen ones, is covered with clinging ivy, twining gracefully around it as if to soften its dark outlines. There the mischief-loving children are hushed in their glee, hurrying feet tread more lightly, more slowly past that sacred spot where reigns a holy calm like the soft breath of prayer. Continuing our walk we enter the summer house built by nature herself, of cypress, which is kept trimmed in the shape of a hollow mound. In this shady retreat are spread, on feast days, sumptuous repasts to be partaken of in true picnic style. Still farther is the Grotto of Our Lady of Lourdes with roses clambering over its mimic rocks and from her niche in the rock over head, our Holy Mother seems to invoke a blessing on all who kneel at her shrine.

But what shady nook is that we see? 'Tis the " Rustic Seat " so well beloved by all the girls. Let us rest beneath the cool shade of the overhanging pepper tree and await the return of the merry boaters, the dripping of whose oars is now plainly heard.

Ah! beautiful home, would that Time and Youth could ever linger within thy pleasant shades! But change, ruthless change, calls many from thy fold. We, too, one day will have to leave thee, to leave forevermore thy sunny bowers, thy dear old walks by the lakeside, thy loved haunts, thy sweet associations, thy dear and happy inmates. But ever in our hearts will we cherish a fond remembrance of the home of our school-days.

KATE CORNELL.

Convent of our Lady of the Sacred Heart, Oakland, Cal.

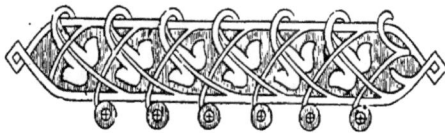

CONVENT OF OUR LADY OF THE SACRED HEART, OAKLAND, CAL., 1868

Art in The Service of Religion

٭

Artists are nearest to God.   Into their souls

> " He breathes His life, and from their hands
> It comes in fair articulate forms
> To bless the world."

God is infinite truth and perfect beauty.   Without the existence of God as infinite truth, science is impossible, for it can never be well grounded, unless it rests upon the eternal and first cause.   As perfect beauty, God is the ideal of the soul in every conception of art.   " There is in man a memory of the perfection with which he was sent forth from the hands of his Creator ; there is also a craving to fashion himself after a picture of his imagination conformable to the idea he possesses of the beautiful—a type combining the first and last excellence of being ; which it is his to enjoy, since he has a conception of it, and to which he ought to be able to arrive, since he aspires towards it.   Thus from remembrance and a feeling of a hereafter is born poetry, is born art ; the expression of ideal beauty under a created form, either gleaming on canvas, breathing in marble, or speaking from the living page."

It is this ideal that wins the love of man, raises him on the wings of contemplation, and bears him aloft toward the Infinite. It gives to Nature its religious power over man, for this ideal is a gleam from the face of God which has penetrated the clouds of the

6   81

material world, and is reflected through the blue heavens, the starry
sky, or whatever is grand or beautiful in nature. "Man is necessarily impressed and ennobled by the beautiful, for there is nothing
sensuous in the idea of true beauty. Its property is to purify
desire, not to inflame. Hence art addresses itself less to the sense
than to the soul; it seeks to awaken not desire, but sentiment.
Chastity and beauty seek each other. Chastity is beautiful, and
beauty is chaste. Therefore, art which is the expression of beauty,
is necessarily moral, elevating and religious." Man feels its influence steal over him, inspiring him with a holy longing to return
to that home from which he has caught one glimmering ray.

Is it not true that all the creations of art aim heavenward?
Each in its own way aspires to perfect beauty. The massive Cathedral, rising above the surrounding habitations of man, points firm
and fearless, straight to Heaven. Silently it proclaims the word of
God and the destiny of man. The marble statue is but the created
form of the ideal form in the sculptor's soul; and the ideal is
always spiritual, heavenly. In painting, music and poetry is seen
the religious tendency and through them runs a vein of religious
sentiment. In them is an echo of the Infinite. In them are strains
of mortal music whose keynote is the rapturous melodies of Heaven.

The true artist seeks after beauty; that only is beautiful which is
perfect, and what is perfect must necessarily be true, good—God-
like. The tendency to the author of all perfection.

Art, I repeat, is necessarily religious. But our nature being
material, it is only by striking the sense that we rise to the spiritual,
and it is thus that art acts as a medium between the soul and the
body; as a chain, a bridge, connecting Heaven and Earth. We
rise by its aid, on the wings of contemplation to spirituality and to
God. When we look upon a lovely scene of nature, or gaze on the
glory of a sunset sky, the soul expands, is overcome with a sense of
the beautiful and is drawn irresistibly to God. It is the silent
homage of the soul to the Creator. It fills us with what we call
"inspiration," and it is in such moments that the poet pours forth

his fullest melody of words, whose mighty thoughts roll out unconscious from the richness of his soul. 'Tis then that the painter seems to have caught a ray from the celestial sun, and the brush in his hand seems to move to the promptings of some guiding angel. 'Tis then that the musician vents the ecstasy of his soul in showers of ethereal melody. Yet in the poet, the painter, the musician, it is the same angel of inspiration that whispers to their souls. This joy, this exultant feeling, has the same cause ; it is the effect of the beautiful, and each one gives vent to his emotions by the power or gift which is prominent in his nature. For Art is an inspiration, and an inspiration can come only from God. And since we love God as beauty, we love God in Art, which is an expression of the beautiful—itself a reflection of God.

Can we then separate Art—the work of the God-like nature within, the incarnation of spiritual sentiment—can we separate it from Religion ?

What seems to prove that Art is a child of Religion, is that never have its creations risen so high as when in her service. Beautiful may be the stately mansion or gorgeous palace, they please and charm the eye. But enter a temple raised to the honor of God, how different the pleasure! Then beauty is of a higher kind. The walls and arches look down in silent eloquence. A something in their solemn majesty commands reverence.

Sculpture peoples the shrines of Religion with myriad saints and angels. Painting grows immortal as it reveals her truths with all their purity and holiness. Religion gives to music that celestial voice which lures the soul to its home above. In poetry she pours a language in our hearts that speaks to the ear of the Infinite.

Thus Art would ever make the visible beautiful, that we might ascend to the beautiful invisible. Art and Religion must then go forth hand in hand—Religion as the inspirer of true Art, and Art as the handmaid of Religion.

ARCHITECTURE.

Foremost among the fine arts stands Architecture. Man in his fallen state built a wretched hut, or scooped out a cave wherein to shelter himself and his family; but when he wished to give worship to the Deity, he erected an altar, decked it with festoons and sought to make it fair. And thus it is through all ages, man has ever had his temples. Under the influence of Religion man has wrought his grandest works; when we gaze on some great mass of stone, chastened and purified by the spirit of holiness that pervades it, instinctively we feel the presence of God. The mind expands when it beholds such spaciousness and strength—the work of man's feeble hand grown strong in faith. And what could profess his faith more loudly than the grand old Gothic cathedral! There the smallest ornament has its religious significance. The triple portal bids us marvel at the mystery of the triune God; the iris-hued rose window recalls his mystical unity. The tabernacle with its silken curtains gives a hint of the sanctuaries of old. The very shape of the church —a cross—is a commemoration of the death that brought life to mankind, and which rests there as a foundation upon which our Holy Religion is built. The silence and gloom of the crypt reminds us of the shadow of death and of the dimness of man's soul when steeped in ignorance and sin. The lofty spire seems a finger pointing heavenward and calling our attention to the glittering cross by which alone victory can be obtained over the powers of hell.

"Ah! those cathedrals of the middle ages pre-eminently bespeak the faith of those times. The wonders of a beauty most sublime and spiritual were not wrought at the decrees of princes, but at the inspiration of Faith and Charity. Entire populations toiled at the sacred task. It is not astonishing that they produced such extraordinary results, Salisbury, Cologne, Strasbourg, Rheims, Paris! On beholding such vast structures, your massive piles, one feels as if the inspiration of a million religious souls had materialized!"

Review those grand structures: Milan looms up as a glorious embodiment of Faith.

Only some angelic spirit could portray its perfection and grandeur. Like some fair mirage suspended in air does it appear, so ethereal and immaculate looking are its thousand pinnacles. One would think that some spirit had thrown over it a veil of driven snow, embroidered and begemmed with myriad jewels, for only thus can one account for the richness and delicacy of this massive pile.

And what of that grandest of temples—St. Peter's at Rome! I shall glean a few quotations—the first from that charming book—"A Sister's Story."

"In Gothic churches our first impulse is to kneel and bow down in humble prayer and deep contrition, while in St. Peter's on the contrary, the spontaneous feeling is to open our arms wide with joy, and to look up to heaven with rapturous enthusiasm. Sin does not seem to crush us there. A consciousness of forgiveness through the triumph of the Resurrection fills the whole soul."

Listen to this eloquent stanza from Byron:

> " Enter, its grandeur overwhelms thee not;
> And why? It is not lessened, but thy mind,
> Expanded by the genius of the spot,
> Has grown colossal, and can only find
> A fit abode wherein appear enshrined
> Thy hopes of immortality."

One more quotation—that very familiar one from Mme. de Staël's Corinne:

> " The architecture of St. Peter's is frozen music."

Ah! yes, I add, it is truly the music of a great and mighty soul. I can well imagine it to be some grand triumphal hymn that has suddenly been stayed in its heavenward flight and transformed into a permanent hymn of praise to God. Thus tower, and spires, and wondrous domes, uprise all over the earth, as silent guides in our wanderings here below, ever pointing out our way to the home towards which we, as pilgrims are traveling.

SCULPTURE.

We love the marble spell of sculpture that binds the ideal of a master-mind almost imperishably before us. Its fairest conceptions are in the service of religion ; it is that very spirit of religion breathed into them that has made them immortal.

As architecture has been styled "frozen music" so might sculpture be called a "frozen poem." It is the giving of form to the conception of the soul. It is one mighty thought, arrested by an angel in its flight through the mind, a conception worthy of being known to other minds, and revealed in all the whiteness of its purity.

Pagan sculpture was beautiful indeed—beautiful because of its proportion, its grace and delicacy ; but that secret beauty which speaks to the soul was unknown; it seemed to lie dormant in the beautiful but soulless forms, as it was in the illumined souls. The Pagan sculptor has not even tasted the living waters of faith and love at the ever-flowing fountains of our religion. Pagan art was the work of the imagination, Christian art of the soul. Gifted indeed, was the hand of Phidias that sculptured the Olympian Jupiter, but were we to compare it with the Moses of Michael Angelo, we would find one lifeless and cold, the latter alive and animated by the breath of religious inspiration. In viewing one we can never forget that it is marble; in gazing upon the latter it is almost impossible to realize that it is merely stone, for a soul seems to have been imparted to the lifeless clay. "There is something infinite in that countenance. The sadness which steals over the face of Moses is the same deep sadness which clouded the countenance of Michael Angelo himself"—the sadness of a great soul that realized in some degree the awful chasm between God, in His infinite holiness, and the sons of men, in their pettiness and folly—an indefinable melancholy and veneration which sought no model and has found no rival.

It was religion that inspired the Gates of Ghiberti "fit to be the gates of Paradise"—the Campanile of Giotto, so delicate and fairy-like that it looks as if "it should be kept under a glass case."

It was religion that guided the chisel of the sculptor, as he peopled with marbled saints every nook, portal and spire of the vast Gothic Cathedral, until, like some holy multitude crowning some fair mountain in heaven, they seemed indeed a celestial concourse petrified in adoration. When Architecture had done its work, Sculpture came in to throw a veil of beauty over the pride of the architect's imagination. From base to finial was added variation upon variation of delicate stone tracery; fine embroidery was tossed and strewed from pillar to vault, and niches were filled with countless angels and saints. Thus in the service of Religion, Sculpture and Architecture ever worked in harmony.

⁂

PAINTING.

Painting, likewise, asks to be received into the temple of Religion. Within the Painter's soul Religion imprints her glorious ideal, and, guiding his brush across the canvas, she aids him to reproduce this ideal. All nature, physical and spiritual, yields to the sway of Painting; from earth to Heaven she wings her flight, portraying all between.

But the painting of Paganism encompassed a far smaller sphere, for it confined itself to the material; above this it could not ascend, for the artist expressed no higher inspiration than that afforded by his imagination, a purely organic faculty. Yes, Religion has imparted to Painting its fire, its soul, and within her hallowed sanctuary have artists executed the world's masterpieces.

See how nobly Religion has employed this art. It is the language of the church. There hung with pictures it is an open book, from which even the ignorant may learn. We need not turn its pages, but only gaze and read in colors the life pictured there.

"Christian painting began in the Catacombs. In the rude pictures of that subterranean world we find the chief doctrines of Religion represented under forms the most touching. Painting there represents the Phœnix rising from its ashes, emblem of the immortality of the soul and the resurrection of the body; the good shepherd bearing upon his shoulders the lost sheep, which teaches with touching simplicity one of the most beautiful of Our Lord's parables; the three youths in the fiery furnace, signifying the Providence of God for those who fear and love him; Pharaoh and hosts engulfed in the Red Sea, proclaiming to the faithful that God is the avenger of those who put their trust in Him."

St. Basil declares that painters accomplish as much by their pictures as orators by their eloquence. Indeed, the divinity of Christ is as manifest in the "Transfiguration" of Raphael as in the famous sermon of Massillon. His sufferings on Mount Calvary are as feelingly portrayed on the canvas of Rubens as in the unequalled discourse of Bourdaloue. No one can look upon the "Last Supper" by Leonardo de Vinci without being inspired with a sublime conception of that holiest event.

Thus the most renowned works of the great masters were ever inspired by Religion—the delicate cherubini of Angelico, the Assumption of Titian, the marvelous improvisations of Tintoretto. To it Correggio devoted his Cupolas, with all their grace and chiaroscuro. Therein Domenichino found his "Last Communion of St. Jerome," the second painting in the world. The Christ of Carlo Dolce and the Madonnas of Sassoferrato and Murillo are in every household. From Religion, Raphael, that prince of painters, drew the epics which compose the Vatican galleries. Not only were his first essays works of faith, but also those which he wrought in his zenith, such as, "The Dispute of the Holy Sacrament," "Heliodorus," and the "Miracle of Bolsena." When he preferred to follow only his imagination, he strayed away as in the commissions

ON THE CONVENT GROUNDS

CONVENT OF OUR LADY OF THE SACRED HEART, OAKLAND, CAL.

for the story of Psyche; but later on he turned himself to the grand "Transfiguration" from the midst of which he passed to behold it in heaven.

And Michael Angelo? I can never cease wondering how in the Sistine Chapel he has portrayed the two extreme points of the life of the human race—the Creation and the Last Judgment.

※

Music.

One step higher in the scale of the fine arts, and the mingled symphony of color, light, and shade, bursts into harmony of sound. Music is the voice of angels speaking to our souls. It is the voice of some strayed spirit exiled from Heaven and doomed to earth to teach man to love and to hope. Wandering and telling of its celestial home, it goes pouring its soul in sounds that still retain the heavenly echoes. Music by its nature tends heavenward; we can almost see those high silvery notes stream upward through the air and pierce the blue sky; then when we no longer hear the strain, it has not died away, but is far beyond on its way to Heaven.

The ancients were wont to say that he who cultivates music imitates the divinity, and St. Augustine tells us that it was the sweet sound of psalmody that made the lives of the monks of old so beautiful and so harmonious.

God is eternal harmony, and the works of His hand are harmonious, and His great precept to man is that they live in harmony. Did not Christ come into the world amid the choral songs of the angels? We can never banish music from His church; it seems to enter there like some gentle spirit, whispering the peace of another world into our souls, next bearing them away on its quivering strains to the throne of the Infinite.

Whoever has enjoyed the rare privilege of being present in the Sistine chapel during the Holy Week when the Miserere is

sung, has felt the immense power of religious music. Do you
know of aught more wonderful than the masses of Palestrina, the
" Stabat " of Rossini, the " Crucifixus " of Bellini? As music de-
velops religious sentiment, so Religion gives to music its highest
themes. To her Haydn, Mozart, and Beethoven, owe their divinest
inspirations.

This age of materialism can give but little to the other arts
whose inspiration is faith: but music brushes away the dust of
everyday life and frees our souls for at least a few moments, from
the sordid cares that disturb it. It lifts our hearts to God, re-
minding us that we will one day behold a vision of beauty and
hear a Celestial music, such as eye hath not seen, and ear hath not
heard.

⇥⇤

POETRY.

And now we have come to the last and the finest of all the fine
arts—to Poetry, the outpouring of an inspired soul. Mighty is the
soul of the architect and the sculptor, beautiful and sensitive is that
of the painter and the musician, but the soul of the Poet far surpasses them all. In one line he erects a temple so grand that well
might he exclaim with Justinian: " I have surpassed thee Solomon ! " He sees beauties in nature of which even Claude Lorraine
formed no conception. Poetry and music are one; music is poetry
of sound, and poetry is music in word. But poetry, though less
sympathetic, has a stronger, more definite power than music. It
appeals more to the mind than to the feelings. It is the music of
the intellect, a music played upon the harp-strings of thought,
whose notes are beauty, harmony and truth, whose ringing strain
is God. And what sublime music that word " God " is to the mind!
In its melody it could dwell forever. It could contemplate for a
life-time that most poetic of words, without exhausting the thought,
the knowledge, the power, the immensity, the sublimity there contained. It is from that word that Poetry springs; she claims a

divine origin, and like a true child ever tends to it. In seeking
God, Poetry winged her flight to the skies, and when in that quest
she naturally soared farthest from earth and nearest to Heaven.
Do you wonder now that Poetry, too, wishes to find a place in the
temple of Religion?

In the world of books is there one grander, more sublimely
poetic than that book dedicated by the inspiration of God—the
Bible? There, where God is apprehended in all His majesty, are
heard the voices of David, the poet king, of Jeremiah, and of Isaiah,
ringing with sublimest strains of prophecy, and pouring forth in
poetry the messages of God upon a listening world.

Has even Poetic Greece in her glory give us poems half so grand
as those of the Hebrew Scriptures? What other muse than Religion
inspired the triumphal hymns of Miriam and Deborah! Of what
else did Job write in that bold imagery, that vividness of expression, combined with master-touches of dramatic art, that stamps
this poem as the greatest in Oriental literature? But though the
spirit of song has fled from Jerusalem it has not departed from the
praise of God. Generation after generation has taken up the refrain,
and through the misty ages of the past—aye, even through the
dimmer ages of the future, do I hear the hymn rising in thanksgiving to God.

And the Angel of the Schools deserved from the lips of Christ
himself these words: "Thou hast well written of me."

Did not the privileged mind of Dante and Milton also receive
their highest inspiration from Religion?

And how often in the silence of his heart and when alone with
his own great thoughts did not the "Poet Priest" of the South
listen to her holy promptings."

Before Religion lent her muse to Poetry, the art lay fettered,
except, indeed, among God's chosen people. Sappho sang of love
to the sounds of her Grecian lyre ; Alceus, of war, infusing patriot-
ism in the breast of his listeners ; but the Christian poet chants
sublimest melodies to the Creator of song, and lays his choicest

gems at the feet of Religion. It was she who whispered to him his theme, and he told her his gratitude when he placed on her brow his nobly earned laurels.

··o◊o··

ELOQUENCE.

Climbing the heights of Parnassus let us greet on our way the golden-tongued Polyhymnia. Of her power who can relate the wonders? She sways the multitude as the mighty wind sweeps over the face of the waters, as it gives a voice to the leaves of the forest, or as it commands homage from the undulating prairie.

True eloquence is always artistic, and we must concede that it holds a high place in the Church of Christ. The Master blessed eloquence and bade it convert the world in the memorable words: "Go ye therefore and teach all nations." Eloquence must be spoken; take from it its voice and you take from it its soul. It is the cry of an impassioned nature, in which love, faith and deep-abiding conviction are enthroned.

In all ages eloquence has played a powerful part in the affairs of man. Demosthenes did more to stay the fall of Greece than all the Athenian valor or Spartan courage. "Let us march against Philip!" was the unanimous response of the people of Athens, after listening to one of Demosthenes' eloquent harangues. Cicero's patriotic eloquence saved Rome from the conspiracy of Cataline. And what has this great gift not accomplished in the arena of modern politics and for the public weal? What if Grattan, Curran, O'Connell had never raised their voices in behalf of the down-stricken Ireland! What if Pitt had not poured forth the eloquent and honest convictions of his mind in behalf of American independence! What of our sympathy for Ireland's Home Rule, had not the Grand Old Man stunned the world with his telling oratory!

If human eloquence can so move the multitudes, what a power must it not have, if we add thereto the purity and holiness wherewith it is accompanied when working in the service of Religion! The church has given to the world the noblest examples of eloquence. With pride she points to the names of Augustine, Ambrose and Chrysostom—Augustine whose mighty wisdom confounded the heretic—Ambrose profoundly and logically eloquent held even the great Augustine spell-bound—Chrysostom of golden eloquence, conquering millions of hearts.

Savonarola with his crucifix held at bay the army of Charles VIII. And what jewels were too precious for the grand dames of Florence to sacrifice at the sound of his inspiring voice!

When luxury reigned supreme at the French Court, the stern, grave oration of Bourdaloue and of Massillon caused the wicked king and courtiers to tremble. Boussuet's masterpieces, grand and majestic, poured forth midst the shadows of the tomb, fell upon the ear of the same pleasure loving Court, sad and solemn as the death-knell warning it of the final dissolution.

Aesthetic France returns to her God at the feet of the great orators of Notre Dame—Lacordaire, De Ravignan, Didon and Monsabré.

And in our own Catholic hierarchy are there not names that shine like stars in the firmament of the church—voices which are the outpourings of faith and love and holy ambition that the world may become better and purer?

If the East is proud of her Bossuet, is not our archiepiscopal city equally gifted?

Oh, for the power to sway the soul, to move it in the paths of righteousness, to raise it from the mire of sin into the high, pure regions of virtue. Oh! for a soul on fire to enkindle a flame in the hearts of others!

··o◊o··

CONCLUSION.

Thus every art, Architecture, Sculpture, Painting, Music, Poetry and Eloquence, has felt and known the sweet inspiration of

Religion, and responded to her in purer tones than it had ever
known before. She has substituted for the ideal myths of Pagan
days the purer vision that Heaven alone can inspire; and instead
of restricting and degrading, as some have ignorantly asserted, she
has elevated and purified every branch of art. Christian art could
not be more perfect than it is—blending all that is fairest and
grandest in nature, with all that is purest and noblest in Religion.

Class of '92

Ina Tibbles   Nettie Dimon   Constance McArand
Julia Reed   Emma Seibert

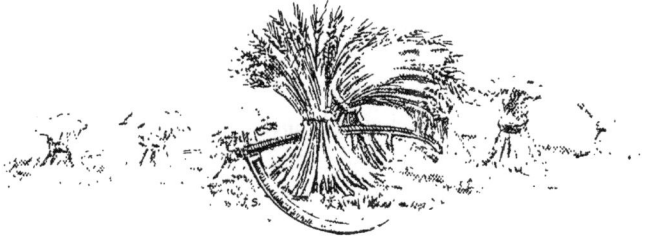

Only a glance from stranger eye ;
A low, soft tone as we pass by—
A curve perhaps, an instant taken
By lips that we to none can liken—

Resemblance, then, with instant touch,
Gives to us thoughts and visions such
As fill our souls for one brief space,
While the heart and its love are face to face.

For other eyes beam then on us,
Too well are known the tones heard thus,
And lips that wore that curve of old,
Words of sweet love to us have told.

K. K.

Seven Years After.

✽

Hath time dealt hardly with thee,
  Child of sorrow, child of tears;
Is the weight of many burdens
  Added to the weight of years?

Have the dreams of school days faded,
  Leaving only memory vain;
All the hope and high ambition
  Given place to weary pain?

Have the weeks and months in passing
  Left but heart throbs in their flight,
Has the dread death angel entered
  Taking all that made life bright?

Has the world been harsh and cruel
  In its coldness and disdain,
Going on its way in gladness,
  Leaving to thy heart the pain?

Have thy shoulders felt the burden
  Of the cross these seven years?
What thy answer to my queries,
  What, my child, tears, only tears!

In the language of the Poet,
   "Tears, the life-blood of the heart,"
Silence only tells the story,
   Words but feebly do their part.

Know you not that all these crosses,
   Are but shadows of the sun,
Whose bright ray will fall upon us,
   When the long day's work is done.

Sink not by the wayside sadly,
   Learn the lesson sorrow brings,
Raise thy heart from earthly honors
   Thou wert made for better things.

Let thy girlhood's high ambition
   To a nobler zeal give place;
All for love, and God's dear glory,
   Till we see Him face to face.

"Whom He loves, He chastens sorely,"
   'T is enough for us to know,
And the word gives sweetest comfort,
   In our pilgrimage of woe.

Courage, for the cross that presses,
   Cometh to thee from above,
And thy Father in His wisdom,
   Sendeth all these things in love.

LAURA J. BRENHAM.

Convent of the Holy Names, San Francisco, Cal.

NIGHT is the dream hour of the day.—*Kate Kenney.*

ON THE CONVENT GROUNDS

CONVENT OF OUR LADY OF THE SACRED HEART, OAKLAND, CAL.

When is the Time to Die?

Life's slowly rising sun purples the eastern sky and tinges with a rosy glow the fleecy, floating clouds. The air is alive with the joyous twittering of the feathered choir; the very brooklets with their sweet babble, seem to laugh and sing, as the sparkling waters ripple along their pebbly beds.

Along the broad and dewy path dances the laughing child. Upon her soft, dimpled cheeks the tints of morning glow. Tripping along she sings sweet snatches of some bright lay. Almost akin to the chirping birds is the blithesomeness of her innocent heart; her light footsteps press the dainty flowers strewn across her sunny way.

I approach the laughing little one with slow and weary tread, and breaking in upon her happy pastime, I cry, "Sweet child, when is the time to die?" The dewy, bright eyes are raised to mine in startled wonder, she seems not to know my meaning. "To die, little one," I repeat. "Is this, do you think, the time to die?" Then her silvery laugh rings out wild and free upon the morning air: "Not yet, not yet!" she cries, and has bounded on again.

The tints of morning have grown more vivid; Aurora has left a kiss upon the maiden's cheek; her soft eyes shine with a loving light; the red lips murmur some loved one's name, to whose memory she is most dear. With the whispered words a flush dyes to crimson her pure white brow. In answer to my solemn question I seem to hear her spirit sigh, as I listen to the words she breathes: "Savior! Oh, not now! not now! Youth is no time to die!"

The soughing wind fans my fevered cheek, and on its wings are borne to me faint echoes of some sweet lullaby. In a little haven by the wayside, sheltered from the storms which ofttimes sweep in all their fury along this path of life, sits a young mother softly crowing to her babe. All her loving heart shines in her eyes as they rest fondly upon the tiny, sleeping face of her cherished first-born. It is with a strange reluctance that I put to her the oft-repeated question—"When is the time to die?" She lifts her eyes, filled with love not unmixed with agony, to my face as she answers—"Surely, not now! God will not call me yet, I have this little life to guide, so that in the end there may be added yet another soul to the numberless saints above." Ah, sweet, unselfish mothers, how you redeem this world! Surely yours is such a noble cause, God will spare you to fulfill your task.

The bright noonday sun is shining steadily in the far, still zenith, whilst along the path with joyous steps and earnest mien, quickly passes a young man in all the fire and zeal of his prime. In answer to the all-absorbing question, he faces me with a look of scorn in his eyes. "Time to die?" he says, while his lip curls in disdain. "Ask that not of me. I have the greater part of my life yet to live! Speak not to me of death, go to age, he can tell you the time to die!"

"Ah, thoughtless one!" say I, as I turn away unsatisfied. The dusk of evening slowly settles over hill and valley. The parting rays of the setting sun gild the distant hills with a mellow splendor; the tall trees cast long shadows aslant the path. In the distance, with his face toward the fading beams, wearily plods an aged man. The tender after-glow touches his flowing locks with a golden glint as he leans on his staff for a moment's rest. He is still standing thus as I draw near. "Tired one," say I, "surely you will tell me now is the time to die." He stands silent for a moment more, then all the ashes of his dead dreams and hopes seem to rekindle in his brightening face; clasping his trembling hands, he cries, "No, no, I cannot die. I love life too well to leave it yet." Poor deluded one! the words have scarcely left the withered lips, when the hand of God silently touches him; a groan, a gasp, and he lies still and cold in the twilight.

Filled with sad foreboding, I continue on my way. Forgetful of all outward things, I speak my thoughts aloud. "Ah me!" I sigh, "why are we all so unwilling to die?" The sound of my own voice in the stillness startles me out of my despondency, and I become aware of a presence near me. Looking up, I see beside me one with a serene countenance and kindly, patient eyes which bespeak the calmness of the heart within. In gentle accents he asks if I am a-weary. What is that light which shines in his face? It is as if a lamp were gleaming with steady light through the windows of his soul. A small, bright hope warms my chilled heart once more. "Thou of the serene countenance," I softly ask, "tell me when is the time to die?" A soft smile passes over his lips and eyes, as if an angel noiselessly floating by, had brushed his face with the shadow of its wings. He lifts his eyes to the purpling west; the mellow light seems to throw a golden halo about his brow as the smiling lips answer: "My Savior's time is mine!"

ZOE CHADWICK.

Convent of Our Lady of the Sacred Heart, Oakland, Cal.

NATURE is the poem of God's love : the stanzas are sound, color and motion.—K. K.

An Arab Tradition

✳

In the midst of the Garden of Eden,
  By the hands of the bright Angels built
Rose a temple of radiant splendor,
  Made of jewels, and sunshine, and gilt.

And the walls were all studded with emeralds,
  In the dome, gleamed the ruby's rich hue;
O'er the cloisters of Peace fell the soft light,
  Through the windows of topaz and blue.

'T was a wonderful structure! this temple,
  As it gleamed in the day's glaring light;
As an emblem of " Peace "—and no Sin—
  It shone like a star in the night.

When the sun o'er that Valley of Eden,
  In the West, at the close of each day,
Sank from sight,—hand in hand our first parents
  To this Temple, came ever—to pray—

And when finished their lowly orisons,
  They would walk through the bright temple hall,
Never dreaming in their sinless beauty,
  That so soon, they would both of them fall.

Adam fell! So the old story tells us,
  Then—this glorious temple of worth
Had its walls rent in millions of pieces,
  Which were scattered broadcast, o'er the earth.

And thus we, from that day have been sinful
   Yet we think that with time, and with care,
We may gather a few of those jewels,
   That were torn from that temple so fair.

*   *   *   *

All ye lovers of gold and of Mammon,
   Who have thought that these jewels so bright
Are for naught but your show, and your pleasure,
   Or to charm you and dazzle your sight—

Let me tell you a secret, I know of—
   That these jewels so rich and so rare,
Are but tokens left here to remind us,
   We've a temple in Eden somewhere.

ADELAIDE C. SPAFFORD.

Convent of Our Lady of the Sacred Heart, Oakland, Cal.

A hidden act of charity sends an irresistible appeal to the Celestial Court of Benevolence.—*K. K.*

God's Music

Like a glorious Te Deum of thanksgiving rose the hymn of Nature to the throne of God; rose in strains of divine melody on that first day, when all things were made good, and a newly created world stretched itself out, decked in its rich robes so fresh from the Maker's hand. A perfection of beauty existed in all things, from the profusion of grasses and gay flowers that carpeted the fertile soil, to the towering mountains, or the billows of the main. And while loveliness smiled its thanks on the face of all created things, a thousand sounds blended into one harmonious whole, and ascended to Heaven. On they chimed, and still they chimed in triumphant chorus, ever praising, ever glorifying the Almighty Power that called them into being.

For if God's name is imprinted in tints of indelible beauty on all the works of the universe, then of whom do their voices sing, and whose music could they call it, if not God's? All sound, every ripple and wavelet of air, every tiny vibration, is God's music.

The universe is filled with His voice. To each of His creations He has given one of His divine notes; and they repeat it so often that, could we but listen as the angels do, we would hear the music of His name in the rushing torrent, and in the peaceful lake, in the mournful winds and in the whispering breeze.

But hush! Everything is so still that the Earth seems to be holding her breath to hear some far distant sound. Ah! 'tis the twinkling of the little star-lanterns as they swing to and fro in the sapphire tent, which they almost hide beneath the maze of their beauty.

We hear God's music also, when the air is filled with the rejoicing hum of insects, that are drinking in the sunbeams, and blowing their tiny horns, as they weave and unweave their mystic dance.

Even the gentle rustle of the leaves, when caressed by the soft breezes, and the sweet notes caroled from hearts hidden beneath pretty feathered coats, are songs of thanksgiving to be wafted to Heaven.

The ocean, the grand and solemn deep! How musical is its calm and steady roar; or again, how harmonious the sounds of its restless and dashing billows! List also to the raging voice of the cataract, as in awful fury it leaps over rocky cliffs, while in its onward rush the waters writhe and foam. How weird, how grand the song of the mighty stream! No power of man ever produced such sounds as these. Onward rides the meadow brook, its laughing waters telling of the harmony of nature, as it vies with the inmates of the forest in singing its sweet "Hallelujah." Ocean, cataract, stream and brook, each fills the air with its music; and now come their offspring, the rain drops. They left us unawares, these fair daughters of the Sea; but now we hear their musical sounds as one by one they repentingly return to the arms of their common mother.

Yes; Nature is all harmony, for it is all love. The songs of the beautiful water, and the winds, with their minor chords mingle in sweetest tones.

Joyfully these psalms of Earth rise to the Eternal Throne, and He who sits thereon, though listening to the songs of the angels can still bend towards Earth; can still receive these humble prayers.

But O my God, there are other strains that rise to Heaven, still more delightful to thine ear! They come from the heart of man; they are the broken prayers he is ever breathing to his Maker; and these strains, up-borne on angel wings, soar above the things of Earth and enter Heaven. Such heavenly music they are that we almost think the angels must have ceased playing on their harps and let their own melody waft to us from above.

This is the music that the Master loves best, whether it be the strong, reliant prayer of man, the patient appeal of woman, or the dulcet lisping of the infant. Rising from the earnest and loving heart, it finds an answer in God's own great Heart.

Class of '91

Ranchita Dibblee   Mabel Reed

Isabel O'Brien   Agatha Sabichi   Lillie Reed

Fanny White   Kate White

Convent of Our Lady of the Sacred Heart, Oakland, Cal.

My Sister?

The golden beams of the morning sun
  Like gladsome creatures on fairy wing
Lit up with a halo the face of one
  Who knelt in rapture before her King.

I gazed ; my thoughts like a meteor sped
  To scenes of my youth on a distant shore,
Where a sister's love had a brightness shed
  O'er my budding life in the days of yore.

Ah ! yes ; from the eyes of her who knelt,
  My sister looked as when she smiled
With all the love that a sister felt,
  On me, a happy, thoughtless child.

Again can I see my sister's look—
  Nor call it Fancy's ardent glow—
She gazes, she speaks, from a precious book,
  As she was wont in the long ago.

VIGILAUS.

Venite Adoremus

❋

It was a perfect night. Not a murmur stirred the starlit stillness, and the pale December moon shrouded in a cold embrace the
sleeping vale of Bethlehem. Upon a distant height rude figures
might be descried stretched upon the cold earth keeping their midnight vigils. Clad in coarse garments and wearing low sandals,
these simple-minded men were types of the Judean shepherd. The
hours dragged on and still they slept, one solitary figure only,
pacing the mountain side, and keeping faithful watch. Suddenly,
a soft light fell upon the heights, slowly and gently, like a loving
benediction it closed around them, awakening the sleeping herds-
men. They were not terrified—they were awed. The crescent
moon had dipped her silver horn a full hour since beneath the
western horizon—the stars were blotted out in the dazzling brilliancy.

They looked at each other in speechless surprise, a gentle peace
falling upon them, as in breathless wonder they waited for some
new revelation.

At length a voice sweeter than music broke the stillness, saying: "Fear not," and then was made known to the humble shepherds the "tidings of great joy." The vision vanished. Far up in
the sky they heard the glad refrain, "Gloria in Excelsis Deo," and
long it echoed in their inmost hearts. When the golden harmony
had "trembled away into silence" and the gray dawn was just
breaking in the east, they arose from their knees, each heart beneath the rude sheep-skin mantles yearning to see the new-born

King. "Venite Adoremus!" they exclaimed, and left the mountain side for the manger.

*   *   *   *   *   *   *   *

What are those long shadows darkening the desert? Three strangers, seemingly kings, traverse the plain, borne each by a huge camel. The first bears the unmistakable physiognomy of a son of the Nile, his dark eyes flashing with expectancy and hope, even through the dimness of three score years; there is in their depths an undefinable longing and yet a holy calm. The second bears the stamp of Hindoo parentage, his great folded turban and white linen garments confirm what his features attest. In the third we see a face in strong contrast with its companions—a face beautiful in mold, and beautiful in the expression of wonderful sweetness and faith. The features are pure Grecian, and unstamped by age or care.

In their hearts these men had long felt a yearning for God, and when the star of Bethlehem shed its pure gleams on their souls they felt an assurance that their longing was soon to be satisfied. A golden chain led from their hearts to the Savior's feet; they felt it irresistibly attracting them nearer and yielding to its sweet influence, they drew nigh unto the Crib. How gladly they responded to the "Venite" that echoed deep in their souls! It was like a bell of untold sweetness rung by angel wardens. The harmony was as a promise of peace and light to their troubled hearts groping in the darkness.

Let us stop to listen for a moment, and through the vaults of twenty buried centuries we may hear sweet voices chiming "Venite Adoremus," the song has not yet died away. In every age, in every Christian country are these sweet words hallowed and sung. Every year as the Christian festival dawns, the Bethlehem star of faith sheds dazzling lustre on each loyal heart, as it once did on the shepherds of Judea, and they, too, re-echo "Venite Adoremus."

Ah! if we would always gladly respond to the "Venite!" but, alas, too often we close our obdurate hearts to the blessed entreaty, and worship not at the Crib of Him who came to seek and to save sinners.

"Venite Adoremus!" in how many care-burdened souls do these words find a responsive chord, which vibrates in exquisite sensitiveness to the awakening touch! For how many hearts benumbed with pain has not this pean of gladness opened the floodgates of tears, relieving sorrow and pointing out a new and higher motive for which to live and to suffer.

" As long as the heart has passions, as long as life has woes,"

will this " Venite Adoremus" bear the same sweet meaning as it breathed to the Judean shepherds on the heights of Bethlehem Christmas night, two thousand years ago.

LUCILE EDWARDS.

Convent of Our Lady of the Sacred Heart, Oakland, Cal.

There are lives that bless and are blessed where'er they go. They are like fertilizing streams that flow through the arid desert clothing its dreary sands with a mantle of softest verdure and gemming it with starry flowers.—*Laura Glenn.*

There are sunbeams that owe their light, not to the sun, but to some golden hearts that cast their fragrance o'er our pathway. When our lives seem cold and dreary, they drive away the gloom. A word, a look, a smile from those we hold dear, brings happiness to many a weary heart.

At the Turning

Just as Time turns to bid farewell to Summer,
  To catch the last perfume she breathes;
Snatching stray bits of her radiance and color
  He paints gray October's sere leaves.

Thus tenderly leaving a seal for a memory
  Of beauty we would not forget.
Blends us a promise in Autumn's own colors
  Of radiance more rare for us yet.

True ! but for Thee all had been cold and dreary,
  Thou hast a mysterious chain,
Which links the beauties of ne'er forgot Summer,
  And in thy gray shadows we live it again.

Just at Time's Turning, we linger a moment,
  To catch the last breath of our flowers.
Take a long look into our fleeting Summers,
  Where Memory and Promise are ours.

There, in the meadows, Forget-me-not faces
  That bloomed in the sweet olden days,
Lovingly peep into ours, and are smiling
  In just the same olden ways.

Then "at the Turning" the birds are all singing
  Sweet snatches of song we once knew.
Looking just back of the Clouds of October
  The Gray melts away into Blue.

Thus, at the Turning of Summer to Autumn
  We look at a picture of Spring,
So, at the Turning of years doth our Memory
  Sweet pictures of childhood then bring.

What of the promise that comes of the blending
  Of Autumn's deep red and rich gold?
'Tis of a Summer where never is fading
  Nor Songs, nor its faces grow old.

For into its meadows, Time never may trespass
  To snatch away Beauty and Light
All the day long we may dwell in the Sunshine
  For there—never cometh the Night.

Memorial pictures of all our past Summers,
  We love Thee ! and most would delay :
But at the Turning of years we're reminded
  Of Summer :—Just over the Way.

And as our years grow more numbered
  They draw us, so gently but surely away
From Memory's Pictures so faded and misty
  To one that is brighter than they.

Nearer and nearer we grow to that Summer
  We oft hear its music, it seems;
And we look through the beautiful blue of its Heaven
  To faces of light in our dreams.

Till at Life's Turning, we pause for a moment.
  Scarce knowing a change is made
Loving and trusting we turn,—and awaken
  In Summer that never doth fade.

ADELAIDE C. SPAFFORD.

Convent of Our Lady of the Sacred Heart, Oakland, Cal.

The Sky

How strange it is that man fails to see in the sky, that ever broadens above him, proofs of the beneficent love of God! Is it not that part of Nature that speaks most eloquently to his soul, that responds best to his heart's noblest thoughts? It is a book constantly open for his meditation; yet, page after page is turned, glory after glory fades unheeded. But let an angry cloud steal over the azure of the heavens and shroud from his gaze the genial rays of the sun, then man is troubled. Perhaps it will mar some pleasure, blast some hope, or even sway the tide of fortune; his mind is full of thoughts darker than the overhanging canopy. Ah! fickle man, who but an hour ago allowed to pass unadmired the glory of a sunset, now watches every movement, every fold that is gathered in the heavy drapery above. But soon the sun-beams find a rift, and as the clouds melt away in the mist of blue rain, man's gloom disappears, and he smiles. A hasty prayer, and again the sky is forgotten.

We are ever awake to the beauty of the hills, to the changing moods of the sea; we trace the delicate beauty of every vein in the hare-bell's cup, and strolling along the sea-shore our eye is ever quick to catch the gleam of some pretty shell. But every one cannot feel the breezy spray from the sea upon his cheek; to some a breath from the ocean's lips would restore new life and strength. Alas! for them, they are far distant from the sound of its mysterious voice. To many, the dainty hare-bells nestling 'mid waving grasses, is a tiny bit of beauty still unknown; but the sky—infinite in its expanse—where will we not find it? Where does it not smile down upon us? It matters not how poor or rich the surroundings, be it hovel or palace, we have but to uplift the eye to meet its gentle downcast glance. There is a charm in its brightness, yet it is not "too bright and good for human Nature's daily food." Ye students of Nature, who love to note each changing aspect of the whispering woods, ye know not what beauties unfold themselves above your heads! Look into the deep blue chasm of the air, study each passing mood! Is not its soft Summer tenderness as beautiful as a mother's smile? Sometimes capricious, sometimes fearful, sometimes gentle—is it not almost human in its passions? Is it not almost divine in its infinity? Yet how seldom do we heed its moods, how seldom do we read the lesson of the sky! We turn not our thoughts thither, and when we so speak of it it is only when a lull in our conversation causes us to complain of the sunless day, or perhaps praise the warmth and brightness of the morning. Who among the group could tell of the great white chain of mountains that girded the horizon at noon, or the little sun-beam that, stealing out, smote upon the melting crest? Yet every cloud that sweeps across the blue above has a lesson to convey, for has not God set His bow in their folds; does He not hide His kindness in their very depths? Each bright ray that leaves the sun bound on its gentle mission is shivered into myriad beams in the misty ether of the sky. Those airy mists that veil yon mountain crest will soon turn to hurrying clouds that skim across the evening sky : and when the parched earth looks lovingly up to the serene heavens they will join their hands across the sky, and 'mid the wail of tempests and crashing of thunder they will drop their "garnered fullness" down upon the thirsty earth. Oh! how appalling is the majesty of the sky in its sterner moods! But as the sun smiles again through a rift in yonder cloud, these cheering words come to the mind : "He shall set his promise in the bow." See it arching its many hues across the heavens : is it not a fit messenger to recall to us God's undying promise? Again, clouds are the ministers of God, for to their care has he entrusted the glorious sun. They spread at morn the golden pavement for His chariot wheels : for

Him they build a temple of dazzling whiteness at noon ; and they draw at evening the purple veil about the sanctuary of His rest. Dancing before the radiant orb of day, they scatter everywhere the sparkling gems He pours from His vast urn ; or, heaped in a snow mass upon the vapory blue, they suggest to us the truth that God, in His wish to be nearer to us, has set His throne in their midst.

But if we have failed to notice the sky and its beauties, others have not. To them the fleecy forms of the clouds tell of Him " who giveth snow-like wool, and scattereth hoar-frost like ashes." Some never watch the evening sky without remembering that those ambient folds of clouds are like the same that enveloped the sacred form of our Saviour, and hid Him from the sight of His loving disciples. How consoling to think that heaven is directly over my head : at night it seems especially near, and when I look up I imagine that the starry veil of the sky is all that is between heaven and me ! But full well do I know that something darker, deeper than the sky, hides from my vision the great White Throne.

Ah ! how many beauties have passed us unseen, unregretted, because unknown ! Let us not leave them unnoticed, but know them every one, for there is a lesson in every leaf, and each phase of Nature is the autograph of God.

ZOE CHADWICK.

Convent of Our Lady of the Sacred Heart, Oakland, Cal.

God alone knows the value of a kind word.—K. K.

ON THE CONVENT GROUNDS

CONVENT OF OUR LADY OF THE SACRED HEART, OAKLAND, CAL.

Apart

What a mysterious little word Apart is !

It holds within its small compass a power which awakens the deepest emotions of a loving heart, and yet, strange to say, it also contains a depth of meaning which brings joy, peace and happiness to the soul.

If we consider it as one word, what may Apart mean ?

These five little letters may tell us that five hundred miles lie between us and the smiles of loved faces !

What may apart mean ? That perhaps five minutes' distance only, separates us from those whom duty keeps from our side !

Apart ! Apart ! It whispers that an idle word, a weighty trifle has severed hearts and lives that should have flowed on as one. Apart ! That word which affection dreads even more than death, that word which friendship is loath to pronounce !

But let me transform its letters into a word of life " A part." What care I " though leagues of land divide us and oceans roll between," if I am confident that within my own breast I bear with me a part of my friend's heart, that I have left with my loved one a part of my own !

What care I though I roam 'neath a foreign sky "a stranger in a strange land," if my soul whispers to me that I have a part in the thoughts of the friend I have left behind ? What care I if sorrow, trials, misfortune assail me when I am certain that there are some who will bear a part of my weighty charge, and lighten by daily prayers a part of my weary burden ?

My soul is cheered on while still in the "Valley of Tears," when I think that though I may be apart from those my heart cherishes a day will come when we will share together a part of Heaven on that bright shore where "sorrow is no more, and parting is unknown."

FLORENCE HYDE.

Convent of Our Lady of the Sacred Heart, Oakland, Cal.

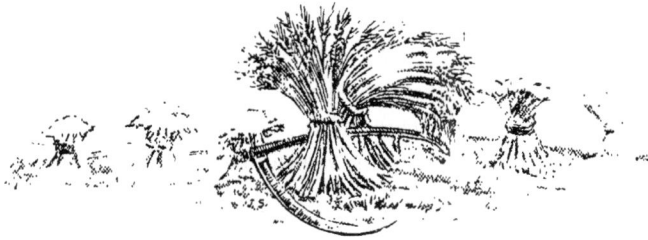

Such is life, first, a greeting to earth and its joys, then, a parting, a sad farewell, leaving behind naught but a fleeting memory.
—*May French*.

❖

O, Lone Mountain! City of Tombs! Well hast thou been named. Densely populated as is thy area, thou still art lone, thou resting-place of the dear departed. Thou art a great book in which we may read the lives of the many who slumber beneath thy sod, and taking unto our hearts thy lessons, wiser grow.
—*Mary T. Dawson*.

To Estelle

※

Perhaps it is a fancy,
But it always seems to me,
That little children earthward sent,
Are flowers from God's garden lent.

Just here a pansy blossom sweet,
And there a violet's dainty face,
While, pure and fair the lily tall,
With blushing rose, fill bower and hall.

The wayward daffodil that nods
And bends to every passing breeze,
The winsome fairies of the wildwood,
Who softly troop like dreams of childhood.

But thou wert Stella, e'en a Star,
Thine eye did ray as pure a light
As comes from seraph, great and bright
Who basks fore'er in God's blessed sight.

The One who sent thee, for awhile,
Kept thy dear heart all for His own,
He knew how soon with brightest beam,
Thy glance should heav'nward dart its gleam.

Earth was not fair enough, Estelle,
Its frame no fitting case for thee,
For thou wert made for nobler things,
A throne befitting royal kings.

Now favor'd one, from thy dear Home
Where crown'd thou stands't harp in hand,
Look down on Mother, Teacher, Friend,
And strains of thy sweet music send.

'Twill soothe the anguish'd heart of her,
Who solaced e'er thy earthly woe,
Who loved thee with an endless love,
And longing waits her call above.

It is the hour of twilight when all earth seems wrapt in a silent spell, it is the hour over which Time loves to linger and to open to the longing eyes of youth the broad vista of the future, ever flavored with the sunshine of happiness. A fair young girl is seated on the rocks, gazing far o'er the sea; the murmuring of the waves as they break upon the strand falls unheeded on her ear, she sees not the beauty of the scene, for her thoughts are far away. The eyes where love lies dreaming and the blushes that softly mantle her cheek, tell that she is wandering in the future's rosy path. It is with a sigh she rises as the deepening shadows of night dispel her visions. O, halcyon days of youth, how heedlessly are you spent! O, child of Heaven, remain not a dreamer; why trouble yourself about the future, 't is all prepared for you by the good God.—*Mamie Lafferty.*

Raphael and Michael Angelo

✳

Which of these two names shall be placed first ? It is indeed hard to decide. Alike only in being great and famous. We need only hear these names, and before us arise two forms, resplendent, transfigured in the light of immortal fame and radiance of their own great souls.

Many are the stars that shine in the vast firmament of art ; many beautiful and brilliant, illuming the earth with their heavenly light ; but these two—Michael Angelo and Raphael—they rule, they are as the great sun and the beautiful moon. When that sun is in the heavens the stars are eclipsed and only his majestic self is visible. But that sweeter light of silvery moon—who would part with it ? It envelopes the earth, and holds it spell-bound in its chains of beauty. Yes, the mellow light from Raphael's brush lures us away ; until, gazing deeper and deeper into his heavenly visions we are unconsciously lifted far, far away, until we find ourselves listening to the melodies of angels that bless the lovely Mother or praise the transfigured Christ. How beautiful must have been the soul that filled that mind with such heavenly images and guided his hand in creating such soulful faces and angelic forms ! He must have lived, not as other men, who ever turn their sight on earth and things of earth, but in a realm of harmony and beauty. One would think that his keen eye had even pierced the azure sky, and the beauty of Heaven itself was stamped upon his soul. Yes, it is only from Heaven that he could have caught so divine an expression as that which breathes from the face of his Madonna di San Sisto. When we look upon it, it is as though by an especial privilege the curtain of earth were drawn aside ; and, behold ! in a real vision of Heaven, the Mother of God radiant. almost dazzling with celestial light.

Ever gazing on the beautiful countenance of angels, his own face seems to have taken the impress of angelic beauty. And, when that beauty was, in all its freshness of growth and fairest bloom : when the young artist's soul was still ardent with the love of the beautiful, God took him where his soul would live for evermore on heavenly beauty : and where, in youthful beauty, amongst the angel faces, his would blend in the harmony of Paradise.

And yet, the prince of painters was proud to consider himself a rival of the mighty Angelo, and to let the influence of this master of art be seen in his own beautiful work. Yes, mighty indeed must have been the man that Raphael was proud to equal. The greatness of Michael Angelo is too great for the human mind to grasp. He holds us spellbound and wondering ; we cannot look the mighty sun in the face : his light is too dazzling for our poor sight ; and we are stunned and blinded by its strength. Like a streak of lightning he flashed through the world of art, crumbling all else to dust and insignificance. But, mighty as are his works, his "Moses," his "David," his "Prophets," these were but a reflection of the mightier conceptions that filled the soul of Angelo. Those indeed must have been stupendous and too great, alas, for the touch of any human hand. Yes, the names of Raphael and Michael Angelo will ever echo in the world of art. It is almost impossible to compare them : both so great, yet neither greater—Michael Angelo, the archangel of painting : and Raphael the guardian angel to the young aspirant of art and beauty.

Their ardent souls at last are satisfied : for now the soul of Michael Angelo can contemplate face to face, a greatness greater than his own great soul: there he can realize his ideals in the infinity of Heaven, and the immensity of God. There Raphael sits, amidst choirs of angels, listening to the enraptured song of his "Cecelia," and ever gazing into the beauty of that divine Mother whom he loved and honored on earth.

INEZ DIBBLEE.

Convent of Our Lady of the Sacred Heart, Oakland, Cal.

Our Pleasant Days

He who replenishes the star-lanterns and hangs them one by one to light up the face of night ; He who scatters flowers abroad over the earth to make it fairer and more fragrant; He it is who twines the pleasant days into man's life. The Poet of our fireside has said:—

> "Into each life some rain must fall,
> Some days must be dark and dreary."

But alas if we consult stern facts, daily experience, shall we not conclude from the average life of mankind that "into some days only, the sun is still shining," "many days are dark and dreary."

At creation's morn all days were days of happiness. Man's life was to be a perpetual sunshine, as it lay untainted in the light and love of the Creator's beneficence. Sin was the first cloud that obscured the sunlight of that glorious day, the first pang of sorrow that pierced a human heart. Ah, what a day to remember. What a day for all generations to regret. And how through the long, stern, penitent years of our First Parents' exile, how the memory of that sinless day, "walking with God in the garden," must have stood apart—a thing of beauty, but no less of pain, lying in the shadow of their offended Maker's displeasure, revealing a claim to happiness wilfully forfeited, and forfeited forever.

Yet they had a Father to deal with, whose mercy and love were not commensurate with His justice, whose Divine Heart could not fail to be touched by the woes of His penitent children. He would not dry up every source of pleasure, nor quench every light that might brighten their pathway. Along the rugged road of life, this forgiving Father has strewn many a pleasant hour, and there are few or none that have not to thank Him for days burdened with the wealth of His gifts, as well as the perfume of sweet memories.

What are happy days? The standard would vary with the capacity and possibilities for suffering and enjoying. Taste, situation, temperament, knowledge, the physical, moral and intellectual conditions of mankind,—all would tend to make the standard differ. The invalid would bless God for a day's freedom from pain; the man of keen moral sensibilities would look for his sunny day among his virtuous and noble deeds; while the saints would soar to lofty summits in the unseen world of beauty and truth. God's unclouded smile is the sun of that Nuptial Feast in which His holy ones revel eternally. The scholar would find it in the domain of the intellect, midst new prospects, lofty thoughts, startling theories; while the child of art would call his happiest day in which he had given expression to his life-long ideal.

But a young girl's happy day, would she find it among these categories? No; the latter, for the most part, lie beyond the field of her experience. She must look back to the days of her child-life, where pleasant hours are as many and luxuriant as the flowers she loves to cull. Without a care, without a sorrow, she is the child of sunshine and song. Walking hand in hand with Innocence and Loveliness, Nature lavishes upon her the beautiful, Religion establishes kinship with the Angels, the Savior leaves upon this age the print of His blessing, and His loving invitation: "Suffer little ones to come unto me." "Oh! how we envy the children," says the Poet, ignoring as they do the Past, smiling at the Present, bounding towards the Future. What are all their days, but pleasant days? Again our Poet sings:

> " What would the world be to us,
>   If the children were no more?
> We should dread the desert behind us
> Worse than the dark before.

Ye are better than all ballads
That ever were sung or said,
For ye are living poems
And all the rest are dead."

The first season of childhood vanishes, to make room for another phase in which the development of reason tempers the glowing atmosphere, wherein the little ones delighted to bask. With the dawn of this faculty and its gradual development, the struggles of the child begin—temper must be restrained, ignorance overcome, good habits instilled, the serious work of life commences, and now the bird which hitherto gladdened us with joyous song gives forth at times a note of sadness; its wings are clipped, its flight impeded; its freedom interfered with. Alas for the caged songster, will it carol no more? Have all its happy days been counted? The child thinks so in the outburst of its first sorrow, beautiful in its very earnestness. But it is a spring-shower merging suddenly into new visions of happiness, and the day is only brighter for the cloud that overcast its morning. "O man thou pendulum 'twixt a smile and a tear," finds ready application in this period of child-life.

Travelling onward the child has reached a more serious phase. Application and learning meet her with an ominous look. They point to arduous duties, to precipitous heights, to rugged paths which must be travelled over ere the goal is reached. Towards that goal the school-girl must ever press—press on as the soldier does towards victory, as the conqueror to his hard-won laurels, for a day of glory crowns the far-off summits. Yonder is her beacon; the clouds may darken, shadows fall thick and gloomy about her, she keeps her eye on this luminary, nerves her will, cheers her oft despondent heart, and presses onward.

Though the journey be long and the task an onerous one, there are many pleasant days strewn along the pathway of school-life—days bubbling over with frolic and mirth—days of quiet enjoyment, of sweet intercourse with master-minds, wherein lofty ideas are formed and " Excelsior " becomes the life-long motto—days of sweet dreaming when everything is fair and everyone worthy of love and trust. Alas that the illusion should vanish, that the charm should be broken.

Leaving the path of speculation and sweet reminiscence, we pass into those of reality. We, dear companions, have climbed those summits, and the day whose light outshone that of all other days, has dawned upon us. In it we see reflected all the joys of the Past, we read the hopes of the Future. Let ours be the song of the vintagers as the grape gives forth its luscious wine, ours the mirth of the harvesters as they garner in the golden sheaves. Whom do we find here to greet us? Those who have gone before us in the race. The friends of our childhood extend a welcome; the loved ones of our fireside press us to their bosom; Mother Church is here in the person of her prelate and pastors to bless us and smile their approval. Oh the joy, the pride of this eventful day, beautiful as it is in reality, will be still more charming in hours of retrospection. We hold it, dear companions ; we bless God, our dear teachers and beloved parents for the long-desired prize. Standing as we do on the threshold of the future, with a pure and lofty ideal in view, we kneel at our Archbishop's feet to beg a blessing that as our lives broaden and sink into deeper channels, our souls may be wedded to useful and virtuous deeds, and that the crown of true womanhood may ever be entwined with the laurels we bear away from our Alma Mater.

FANNY WHITE,   KATE WHITE.

Convent of Our Lady of the Sacred Heart, Oakland, Cal.

The lapse of years softens the sorrows and trials of other days.
—*May French.*

The Isle of Dreams

※

In Fancy's em'rald shimmering sea,
　There floats a fairy golden isle,
Whose banks of broider'd clover lea
　On merry laughing waters smile.

This isle of dreams is beauteous wrought
　With loveliness from poet's theme,
Echoing soft, sweet Music's thought,
　Glowing with the artist's theme.

There Nature weaves her fairest charms ;
　Sweet flowers adorned with iris hue
Do waft to zephyr fragrant balms,
　While shy they droop with kiss of dew.

Tall trees their leafy tassels swing
　'Neath gentle touch of nightingale,
Whose lute responsive wooings sing
　To pearly fountain's murmuring tale.

There, veiled in clouds of lace, the morn
　On azure curtained throne appears,
While round her soft, with mystic tune,
　Doth steal the " Music of the Spheres."

Upon that isle Stern Death is kind,
　He brings us back our loved ones gone ;
And hearts on earth that breaking pined
　Are there no longer sad, forlorn.

For oh ! our cherished loved ones dear
   Are with us on that golden shore,
And joy in rapture sheds soft tear
   To know we're with our loved once more.

There, cold earth fades and all is bliss ;
   There, Mortal's spirit Care—is Rest—
And with tranquillity's soft kiss
   It gently slumbers on its breast.

That isle I ever love to roam,
   And there from earth I blissful stray,
For oh ! Love calls it: " Home, Sweet Home,"
   And there it fondly steals away.

Ah ! yes, upon that lovely isle
   Love breathes soft mystic strains ;
No heart aches 'neath its gentle smile,
   No silent sighs, no sad refrains.

With sweetest song she wakes her lyre
   To soft, ecstatic, tender thrills,
Hushing every tone of dire,
   In its warm heart music trills.

Then blame me not if oft from care
   I stray upon that mystic isle ;
For ne'er Earth's sorrows could I bear,
   If there I found not sweet Joy's smile.

EMMA GOETZ.

Convent of Our Lady of the Sacred Heart, Oakland, Cal.

————————

The very consciousness that the good opinions of others are unmerited, causes one to resolve to be worthy of them.—*K. F.*

The Marble Waiteth

✦

Chisel in hand stood the artist—before him a huge block of marble, like a great white cloud about to assume some fantastic shape. Before the sculptor's imagination was passing a long train of fancied images. What a strange picture they made! And what a mingled and grotesque assembly! He must be very near Olympus. See! the form of beautiful Venus following that of a vestal virgin; an inspired Pythoness led by a fearfully beautiful Medusa; a dying gladiator and a lost Pleiad. What mean these varied forms! The sculptor knew not what scene to carve from on the waiting marble. He called upon the gods of Olympus to inspire his heaven-born genius. He prayed ideal creatures to speak to his listening soul. Did his soul catch the answer? Not from Olympus, for the Olympus of Mythology was but a dream. As he stood breathless, expectant, his listening spirit caught the sound of a chant from the ivied cloister on the bluff. He strained every nerve to hear the whole-souled harmony—he felt it thrill through him; he felt the depth of its music; he felt the inspiration it spoke. It told him of a dying Saviour, a sorrowing mother, a repentant Magdalene--Angelo carved his Pielâ.

> " Sculptors of life are we
> As we stand with our lives uncarved before us"

waiting pure and fair as the sacrificial mists that rise from the altar of earth to greet the morning, are our lives, as yet unscathed by sin and sorrow, unlined by care. While we are standing, chisel in hand, to shape the marble before us, false dreams of earth's delusions, bright visions of pleasure, of delight, fairy fire-flies of fancy, sparkling for a day, float in the vista of our imagination.

Let us seize not these delusive charms, but wait—wait, with listening soul, for the psalm of destiny. The zephyrs of prayer will waft to our soul its mystic music; we will catch the strain as it floats from heaven. Upon the waiting marble let us chisel with a firm and steady hand the outlines of true and noble lives. Let us be faithful to the divine inspiration, and upon the yielding stone trace a form that we will be proud to submit to the Master Artist.

> " Let us carve it then on yielding stone,
>   With many a sharp incision:
> Its heavenly beauties shall be our own—
>   Our lives, an angel's vision."

LUCILE EDWARDS.

Convent of Our Lady of the Sacred Heart, Oakland, Cal.

We are cradled in the star-hung world, watched and warded by angels, bearing the image of God, and preparing for a destiny, of whose glory thought has no image and language no name.

—*Lulu French.*

The Trinity Revealed in Nature

❊

When Almighty God placed us on this earth as at a resting-place on our way to our heavenly home, He spread over and around the stern realities of this transitory life a bright veil of delightful mystery, implanted within our souls the desire to enjoy its fascinations and gave us the power of instructing ourselves in the ways of the Creator. Nature is a book open to all, no blank pages do we meet when perusing it, but pages closely written. In it we read of God, of His goodness, His power, His perfections, His love. It is so related to the mind of men, that it is evident they were made for each other. The greatest, the purest pleasures we derive here below are from the contemplation of Nature; but a higher purpose than present pleasure is accomplished; entering life as a germ the soul expands into intelligence, virtue and knowledge through the teachings of Nature, the wisest, gentlest, and holiest of teachers. Creative wisdom never works in vain or in sport. Even the flying cloud has its mission; its fantastic forms and gorgeous colors are divinely appointed. The hills and valleys, mountains and dales, which seem scattered in accidental confusion, have received their contour by design; consequently, each stone and mineral composing these hills was also the work of special direction according to ends foreseen. In the living kingdom of Nature, too, there must be an adequate purpose and end accomplished by every movement, and in every creature of the Divine Hand.

Hence, the study of Nature does not only please, but it instructs, as it enables our intelligence to recognize Divine Intelligence. Nature is all luminous with the Divine Presence. It brings the operations of the great Architect almost within the grasp of human intelligence, revealing the conceptions of His Mind before they were embodied in actual existence. We hear His voice in the rolling thunder, contemplate His immensity in the vast ocean, feel His power in the mighty torrent, and adore His love, beauty and goodness in the surpassing wonders of Nature. Nature is a limpid stream which reflects in all its favored loveliness, the most glorious of panoramas. Shall we not gaze into its pearly depths, and read with rapturous admiration and deep reverence the grand secrets which none but the Creator can communicate ? If some in the contemplation of its beauties have been unfortunate enough to forget their Author and wander from the path of truth, can we blame Nature for it ? No, certainly. For Nature, with her waving forests, verdant hills, fertile valleys, and countless rivers, stands as an image of its Creator—and this picture is one we see in almost every substance, animate and inanimate.

It is not my object now to speak of the relations between God and Nature, to define the Trinity, or to explain this first mystery of our Holy Faith, for I have not the capacity required ; moreover, the doctrine of the Trinity is such an incomprehensible mystery, that the more we meditate on it the more wonderful and inexplicable it seems. It is a most sublime revelation, solving the numerous difficulties against which the ancient philosophers struggled in vain. The great St. Augustine, who has written fifteen books on the subject, says in the Conclusion : " But among the many things I have now said, there is nothing that I dare to profess myself to have said worthy of the ineffableness of the highest Trinity, but rather confess that the wonderful knowledge of Him is too great for me, and that I cannot attain to it." Then he concludes by a prayer, beginning with these words : " O Lord, our God, we believe in Thee, the Father, the Son, and the Holy Spirit, for the Truth would not say, Go, baptize all nations in the name of the Father, and the Son, and of the Holy Spirit, unless Thou wast a Trinity." In his work on the " City of God," Vol. 1, Book xi., he consecrates several chapters to this subject, to which we may refer if we wish to study the matter.

Every effect has within it some degree of perfection which gives to it a certain resemblance to its cause, at least analogically. As the artist seeks to leave on the canvas an image of what exists in his mind, so has God left in Nature an impress of the Trinity. Bourdalove, in one of his sermons, said that " there is no mystery where God is more incomprehensible than the mystery of the Blessed Trinity." At another time he said : " I have said it, and again avow it, that the act of religion by which we confess that three persons make one, is the greatest effort of faith." This every one will admit, but we must also acknowledge that no truth is so frequently and in so fascinating a manner presented to us. Almighty God, knowing the pride and stubbornness of man, who will seldom admit what he does not understand, has like an indulgent Father placed before our eyes proofs, as it were, of the Trinity. With wonderful love He smiles on us at every step ; we can not even speak, think, or act without being ourselves images of the Trinity. No teacher is so successful as he who lets his pupils believe that they have the merit of having discovered what his teaching alone has accomplished. So it is with Almighty God ; He has everywhere placed before us images of the Trinity, that we may have the pleasure of discovering these types of their Author. Father Faber says : " As the image of God's perfections, Creation was the faint shadow of that most gladdening mystery, the Eternal Generation of the Son." As the communication of His love, and the love of His own glory, Creation also dimly pictured that unspeakable necessity of the divine life, the Eternal Procession of the Spirit. " Perhaps all the works of God have this mark of His Triune Majesty upon them, this perpetual forthshadowing of the Generation of the God and the Procession of the.Spirit, which have been and are the life of God from all Eternity." Nature, grace and glory may thus perhaps all be imprinted with this mark of God, the emblem, the device, the monogram of the Trinity in Unity. The natural joy of beautiful scenery, the strong grace of Christian holiness, and the thrill of glory which passes from our souls from the unveiled face of God, all draw us home to the Blessed

9

Trinity, our last End and First Cause. "A triple cord of His presence is bound round all things, and penetrates through substance by essence, by presence, and by power." In the kingdom of Nature there are three separate worlds, which are full of exquisite enjoyment : the physical world, which is an emanation from the everlasting and inexhaustible gladness of the Most High ; the intellectual world, with its marvelous shadows of the incomprehensible joys of God himself ; and the moral world, representing Him who is the co-equal limit of the Godhead, the third person of the Blessed Trinity,—and yet these three worlds, the physical, intellectual and moral, are one world, a most striking picture of the Trinity. The threefold heavens proclaim the Trinity. The earth, the sea, and the air form a temple by means of which we are to mount to that glorious kingdom where reside the blessed. Our sources of light are three : sun, moon and stars, that in obedient and majestic harmony tread the path which God has appointed, and move as one, never sleeping. Every great thing is triune. Of intelligent beings there are three orders : God, angels and men. Of created beings, three more : angels, men and brutes. Man is triune in almost every respect. First, his mind—"The mind of man," says St. Augustine, "who knows himself and loves himself, and the mind that knows itself, through itself is another image of the Blessed Trinity. These three are one and also equal, viz., the mind itself, the love, and the knowledge of it ; they exist substantially, are predicated relatively, and are inseparable." There is another trinity in the mind of man, which appears much more evident than the former, viz., his memory, understanding and will, which are not three minds, but one mind. The body of man consists of three parts : head, trunk and limbs ; each limb three members, also three joints. In his face, three features of sense : eyes, nose and mouth ; and three other features ; forehead, cheek and chin. Our lives consist of three stages : youth, manhood and old age. Living creatures are of three kinds : birds, beasts and fishes ; they move in three ways : walking, swimming, flying ; and have three modes of subsistence : carnivorous, herbivorous and omnivorous. There are three classes of savors : bitter, sweet and sour. Actions are of three classes : good, bad and indifferent. Truth also has three divisions : metaphysical, logical and moral. And so on throughout all the universe.

Almighty God has, indeed, everywhere so written the proofs of the Holy Trinity, that he must be very stupid who does not see them. The philosophers have divided philosophy into three parts : physical, logical and ethical—not, however, with any allusion to the Blessed Trinity ; but it is certain that in these three great general questions all their intellectual energy was spent. Again, there are three things which every artificer must possess in order to effect anything—nature, education and practice. Nature is to be judged by capacity ; education by knowledge ; practice by its fruit—the natural having respect to Nature ; the rational to education ; the moral to practice.

St. Augustine finds a picture of the Trinity in love—he that loves, the object loved, and love ; one also in sight ; another in the holding, contemplating and loving faith temporal ; besides many kinds of trinity, too numerous to mention. In the kingdoms of Nature, animal, vegetable and mineral, we have a trinity connected by another, sponges, zoöphytes and diatomes ; the mysterious chains which unite them add a new chain to the study of Nature. In many plants we also find a picture of the Trinity. St. Patrick found one in the shamrock, and used it to instruct the natives of Ireland in that mystery. No number is repeated oftener in the Holy Scriptures than the number three. There have been three dispensations of truth : the patriarchal, the Jewish, and the Christian. There are three divisions in the Old Testament : the Law, the Prophets, and the Psalms. St. Paul mentions three heavens. Adam and Noah each had three sons. There were three great patriarchs : Abraham, Isaac and Jacob. The camp of the Israelites was threefold. Moses appointed three cities of refuge. Three orders served in the temple : high priests, priests and levites. The high priest wore a triple crown. The levites were of three classes. The Israelites had to assemble in the temple three times a year. There were three great religious festivals. According to Holy Scripture, God has regulated all things in measure, number and weight, thus revealing another Trinity. In the New Testament, three wise men came from the East to adore the Infant Jesus. The child Jesus was found in the temple after three days. Three apostles were with our Saviour at the Transfiguration, and three in the garden of Olives. There are three that give testimony in heaven: the Father, the Word, and the Holy Ghost, and these three are one. There are three Theological virtues: Faith, Hope and Charity. While remaining in this world we have three important duties to perform: to God, to our neighbor, and to ourselves. Three eminent good works: almsdeeds, prayer and fasting. Three evangelical counsels: poverty, chastity and obedience. In the Church of Christ, three orders: militant, triumphant and suffering. Observe a triplicity in rational speech: the voice, the word, and the breath. See it again in human existence: to be, to do, to suffer. Matter is disposed in three states: solid, liquid, and aeriform. There are three primitive colors: yellow, red and blue, for by the mixture of these all others are produced, and when blended they form clear white. In the human act there is a triplicity: thought, word and deed. In every syllogism, three parts. Three is an emblem of strength—a threefold chord is not easily broken. The triangle is of the utmost importance in mathematics. Time has three divisions: past, present and future. Our day is composed of three parts: morning, noon and night. The poets take cognizance of the number three. Milton speaks of "three-bolted thunder," and his expression "thrice happy" has a superlative meaning. "In all religions," says Brownson, "in all philosophies, in all thought, in all speech, we find asserted in some form the essential Triad, or the mystery of the Trinity." Even in the fables of Polytheism we find numerous traces of the Trinity. There were three principal deities—Jupiter, Neptune and Pluto. The Greeks divided their gods into three classes—celestial, terrestrial and infernal. They often represented their animals as having three heads. There were three Graces, three Gorgons, three Fates, and three times three Muses. The Romans formerly sacrificed three victims at the establishment of leagues and truces. The Celts and Goths had their triads of gods. The Druids found a trinity in the mistletoe, because its leaves and berries were formed in clusters of three united in one stalk. The divine triad of the Persians was represented by a large circle, in the center of which was the upper part of a human figure joined to the body and wings of a dove. The circle emblem of eternity represented their supreme being; the human figure and the dove, thought, word and action. The Chinese attach a mystical importance to the number three. The Egyptians also had a notion of the Trinity. The Magi were a sort of trinity. Plato seems to have had some idea of the Trinity, as we see by his second letter to Dyonisius. The doctrine of the Trinity is known in the East Indies and Thibet. Many missionaries state the infidels whom they instructed had a faint knowledge of the Trinity. Thus it is at every step, in every clime, and at all ages, Man has lived, and is now living in the very shadow of the Trinity. Let the so-called scientific men of the age deny the existence of the God who created them ; let them lose themselves in the labyrinths into which false science has led them; they can not, no, they can not help feeling in their inmost souls the impenetration of the Triune God. His presence is proclaimed in every particle of matter around us. The bright spark of Intelligence within us is but a ray thrown off from the glorious refulgence of the Almighty. Ah! then, let us not forget our omniscient origin. While wandering among Nature's treasures and blissful meads, let us remember the Invisible Cause, and wait patiently for the time when the mysterious veil will be thrown aside, and we will find ourselves in the ever-shining, gladsome, loving, eternal splendors of the Divine Trinity.

KATIE A. CARR.

Convent of Our Lady of the Sacred Heart, Oakland, Cal.

This little poem is supposed to have been drifted from the blue above, where a loved soul has found anchorage.

An Answer to Christian Reid's "Regret"

✛

If thou hadst known, O loyal heart,
That soon, so soon, the shadows fell,
Thou couldst not then have played a part
More kindly just ; the thought still lives,
Through all the days remembered well,
Within the sacred guard of one,
    Whom thou hast known.

Whom though hast known, yet scarcely knew,
For all the tenderness that dwelt
Beneath the outward calm so true,
Told naught of hidden depth, so felt
That slightest tone, or speech of thine,
Had power to stir the soul of one,
    Whom thou hast known.

No matter where thy pathway hies,
To strange, mysterious land unknown,
Or full in God's bless'd presence lies,
Thy thought will linger round the Throne
And there 'twill be my sweetest prayer
To link thy name, with that of one,
    Whom thou hast known.

For loyal e'er I've been, and long
And constant still my heart shall be ;
No earth-born chains are half so strong
As links formed by eternity.
Now, all the years which love may give,
Thy mem'ry sweetens for the one,
    Whom thou hast known.

O friend, look up, and mourn no more,
The whitening clouds that o'er thee roam,
Are but the snowy, golden floor
That hides from mortal gaze the dome
So steadfast blue that bends and bids
Thee smile and comfort find, in one,
    Whom thou hast known.

For hearts grow strong through grief and pain,
The mystic crucible is this
That purifies from earthly stain,
And love grows fair and does dismiss
All dross ; it brightens in the light
That shines on thee and on the one,
    Whom thou hast known.

Thy hand across the gulf of years,
A pledge of thought that bridges space,
A token now that knows no fears,
That thrills our souls as they embrace.
Awake to knowledge of the truth,
That I am still the faithful one,
    Whom thou hast known.

Ramona

❖

"O south-land, O dream-land, with cycle of green
    O moon-light enchanted by mocking-bird's song;
Cool sea-winds, fair mountains, the fruitland between
    The pepper trees shade, and the sunny days long
    O land, of my love, in thy heart may I rest."

The very name brings a perfume of almond and orange blossoms—while one sees clinging to each support the tender grapevines, festooning themselves in a thousand fantastic forms—away in the distance stretch the thickets of wild mustard.

Look at this beautiful picture of that Home so graphically described by Helen Hunt: "Its windows open on the garden, and the doorway faces the east." "Between the veranda and the river meadows, all was garden, orange grove and almond orchard; the orange grove always green, never without snowy bloom or golden fruit; the garden never without flowers, summer or winter; and the almond orchard in early spring a fluttery canopy of pink and white petals. On either hand stretched away other orchards,—pear, peach, apricot, apple, pomegranate, and beyond these, vineyards. Nothing to be seen but verdure or bloom, or fruit, at whatever time of year you sat on the south veranda."

Does not this vivid picture portray the features of every land·scape throughout the magnificent Southern valley which yields with the luxuriance of the fabled age—fair Garden of the Hesperides with its wealth of magic golden fruit, guarded not by the dragon of old, but by myriads of angels hovering with a special delectation o'er the valley of Los Angeles.

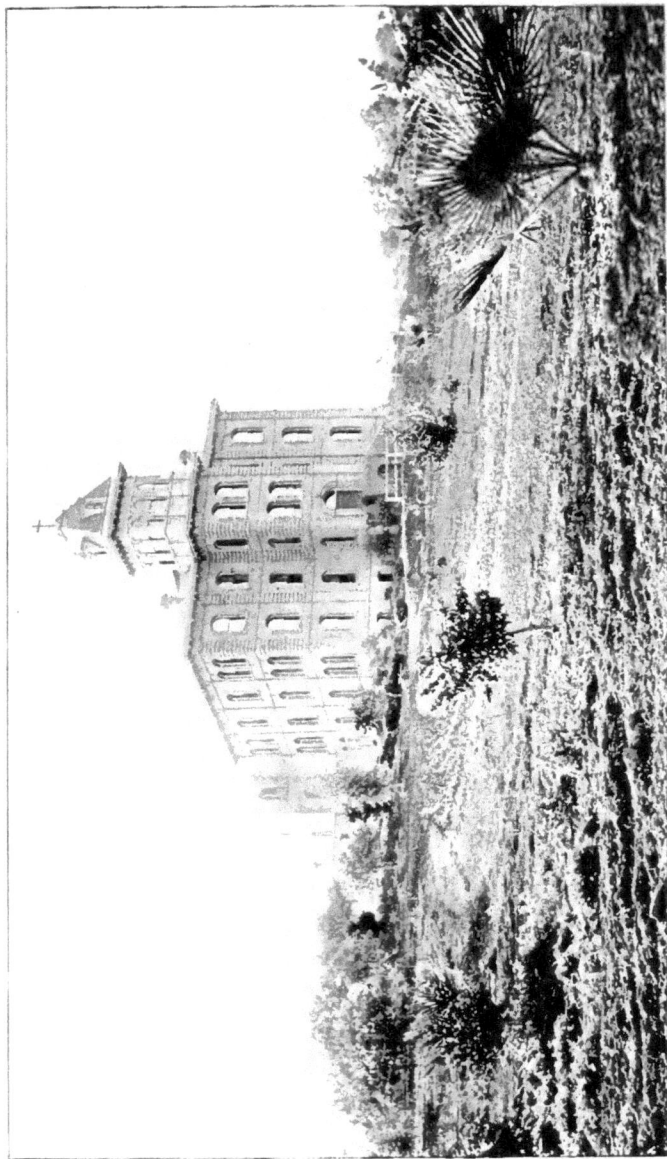

CONVENT OF THE HOLY NAMES OF JESUS AND MARY
RAMONA, LOS ANGELES CO., CAL.

A thrilling sadness lingers round thy name O Ramona, causing one to pause and wander back to the early days of California, when the dusky sons of the forest were rulers of the sod. Scarcely a tract of land that does not teem with reminiscences of this period ; like a chain, the Missions link themselves through the land; each in itself placed where Nature's smiles are fairest.

Just within call of the silver chime of the old San Gabriel, a new city has risen, bearing the name of Ramona, her highest eminence crowned by a Convent, filled with busy workers—courageous successors of the toilers of old. Yonder San Jacinto lies purple and hazy in the distance, while snow-capped "Baldy" keeps constant guard over the peaceful valley so quietly resting below.

Fair Italy with her far-famed mountains and picturesque sites is alone a rival of this gem of our Californian land—

But fairer than the blossoms of the south are the souls of little children, and our clime so favored in every respect lacks not this crowning. Guide then these little feet, O sister-band, that they falter not—lead on to the portals of Heaven, and this our Home, will truly be the vestibule of Paradise.

I often wonder if after all old memories have more of joy than of pain? 'T is sometimes hard to revisit scenes of happier days.

—K. F.

The First Religious Festival in Ramona

※

Never did a more promising day rise on Ramona's fair brow. Never did her verdant fields, sunlit hills and hoary old mountains appear more exultant than in the glow and beauty of her first religious festival. Heaven's blessing and Earth's loveliness blending in one jubilant harmony, over which floats the grand voice of the Catholic Ritual which makes of this a day of golden memories which will ever be sacred to the pupils of this school and to the inhabitants of this part of the valley. For the first time the representative of Christ stands with uplifted hands, as the Savior of old, to call down blessings on the little ones of the flock ; that was a hallowed festival which dawned in the Jewish heavens eighteen centuries ago, and now Christ's prelate has repeated with heart and voice the Master's wish that the lambs of the fold should be guarded from all contaminating influences. For what should our children be, but angels with upraised hands, calling down heaven's graces on the family ? And what greater power is there with God than their childish innocence ? The philosophers of old called a man great, when, with his gray hairs he had preserved all the freshness and beauty of his childhood's heart. So our girls and our women will be great and their influence will be ennobling, if, from their pious teachers in the cloister they learn, notwithstanding the corrupting influences that vitiate the atmosphere which surrounds them, to keep their hearts and mind unsullied.

Echoes of the Past ; how harmoniously they blend with the realities of the Present! Looking back through the vista of years, a quaint but hallowed picture meets our enraptured gaze, in the simple, zealous Padre, the untutored Indian, the quiet grazing flocks—

all making a strange contrast with this busy, progressive age of ours. Yet, the grand Catholic principle, the yearnings of dear Mother Church for the salvation of souls, underlie all this rustic simplicity.

To-day we ascend to a higher plane. Forms have become more refined, culture more sought after ; still we cling to the teachings of the old faith, that Religion and morals are the basis of the social fabric, without which education is a mere sham, and without which, woman, who has such a grand part to play in the regenerating of society and in the raising of the moral standard, utterly fails in the task which has been allotted her by Divine Providence.

We trust, therefore, to realize this ideal, in the young ladies who go from beyond the portals of this Institution.

We thank your Lordship most heartily for the high solemnity you have lent to this festival. We thank the generous donors who have contributed to the building of this Institution ; the Rev. Clergy, friends and acquaintances, who have enhanced the importance of this occasion by their kind and friendly encouragement. We thank one and all for this lovely day on Convent Hill, which will ever be " a thing of beauty " in our reminiscences, and therefore, in the words of the poet, "a joy forever."

Read by MISS EDITH SHORB,

On the occasion of the Dedication of the Ramona Convent.

I Wonder

Pray tell me, philosopher dreaming.
　Or scientist learned and wise,
What is the wonderful beauty
　That shines in the baby's eyes?

We all love the little darlings,
　And none of us know just why,
I fear you lovers of learning
　Are too wordly to guess if you try.

And rocking the tiny cradle
　With a lullaby soft and low
The answer came like a whisper
　To the secret I longed to know.

The depths of the wee eyes vision
　A glimmer of turquoise blue—
A patch of heavenly brightness
　Dipped in heavenly dew.

The baby's smile is surely,
　A beam of the sunshine of love,
Caught in its wings as it fluttered
　To earth from its cradle above.

The meaningless lisp of the baby,
　Is all it remembers quite,
Of that story of peaceful promise
　It sang the first Christmas night.

I know now why these spirits
  Of wonderful baby-land,
Creep into our hearts and boldly
  Their tenderest love demand.

You are dear little cherubs of Paradise,
  Lost in a world of sin ;
And our truest peep of God's glory,
  Is the glimmer that you bring in.

LUCILE EDWARDS.

Convent of Our Lady of the Sacred Heart, Oakland, Cal.

Behold the mother surrounded by her children, these golden links in the chain of Love that bind her to the earth, but the fetters are pleasant and not again for wealth untold would she be free. As she and her little ones watch the dusky shadows of night falling upon the earth, I mark that the mother keeps the thoughtful eyes of the maiden and the happy smile of childhood's bright day. As they gaze upon the stars that come forth one by one and she tells them of that Home beyond the skies, the little eyes are filled with wonder and the little hearts with awe. Later with unutterable tenderness and a silent prayer for her darlings, she bends over them as they lie in the slumbers of innocence, then kneeling, how fervent is her prayer! Self is forgotten—her only cry is for her children. How steadfast, how tender, is a mother's love. Truly has it been said "it is like no other love." How patient with us in sickness, how true in misfortune's dark hour! Her heart is our asylum in our troubles, her counsel is as balm to the heart seared and scorched by passion's stormy breath. O ye Mothers, shall your Children ever know the tears that you have shed for them, the pains you have endured for them, or the swords of sorrow they have plunged into your hearts! Ah, never! God alone knows and to Him your sufferings are as pearls beyond price.—*Mamie Lafferty.*

Spiders

When Summer comes, and the days are warm and dreamy, perhaps you will decide to go to the arbor and be lazy. You acknowledge that you have an especial fondness for this arbor so shady and quiet, and apparently the Spiders are fond of it, too; for there are thousands of them there, with whole villages of their webby homes stretched in the foliage around you.

There happens to swing amid the shadows of this peaceful arbor, quite the dreamiest of hammocks, and, as you lie entangled in it, looking like an entrapped butterfly in a colossal spider-web, you slowly, half unconsciously begin a mute friendship with those queer, black, ugly things that everyone abhors—the Spiders. Soon you begin to " weave a web of similes "about them, and in that web they grow like so many things, and take so many forms, that you almost doubt whether they will ever appear to you again the plain, old, ugly things that you went through childhood fearing.

Now and then you feel quite compassionate toward Spiders, and think them abused and ill-treated far oftener than they deserve, though you acknowledge that at times, they certainly look and are most villainous. You are even quite prejudiced against a certain class that live in those irregularly pitched, dusty, cat-a-cornered webs, for these Spiders always seem to be making eyes at passing flys, and plotting murderous assaults upon them; or planning schemes for kidnapping young and innocent insects. To this despicable set, also belong what you call Witchspiders, for there are some that look wonderfully like witches, as they sit at the door of their little round cells, with their weird fingers stretched out over their webs, in which you think they must weave strange stories, fates and fortunes, which they spread out to tempt the unwary winged traveler to pause and read. Alas for him if he does, for he will never go forth again to reveal them!

But the other Spiders! those that build fine skeleton webs, round in shape, which they generally weave over open spaces. This class you are sure must be of higher instinct. You love to watch their lovely webs so patiently, skillfully and beautifully woven. You look up and see them now stretched over bits of light that seem to be condensed as they pass through the thick foliage, and grow brighter. so bright, that they seem to your fancy, miniature suns in a sky of green ; and the Spiders like mimic transits, as they move in their webby orbits over the suns among the leaves. You certainly take great pleasure in watching these spider-transits, and you are always calling these leg-radiating stars, "queer things." You have just turned and made yourself quite uncomfortable in your hammock, to get a better look at one of the "queer things," that is languidly strolling over the woven floor of a web quite close to you. What mute enjoyment he seems to be taking in the gauzy perfection of his "web-spun castle in the air." You feel quite sad when you think of some thoughtless wind, or heedless hand ever destroying it ; and yet how many webs just as beautiful, seem ever doomed for destruction : but soon the patient Spider will weave a new web over the ruins of the old. Ah, this is a long, long thought for you, so long, that though the shadows have begun to lengthen, they fall upon you unheeded ; nor do you see them weave themselves into a criss-cross web upon the ground, and in that web they play with your shadow image entangled there. Still you look as if you felt the influence of some binding charm, you are so quiet, so thoughtful.

You may have finished your long, long thought, perhaps only to begin another. O bewildering Spiders! they are a puzzle of legs and webs, but you are determined to solve it. But not now, for the twilight has come and is quickly putting away the webs and shadows into the dark, and your thoughts about to finish their ramble, have come home like tired birds from their fancy flight among the webs and Spiders, weary, silent. Ah, they will be wiser birds to-morrow and stay at home, and then perhaps they will sing you an oft repeated song of "hopes and fears" which will bring you back to Reality, that you may there recall that half-forgotten, half-woven web,—your life. Sacred web of thoughts and acts, is it ever to lie tangled with hopes and fears? Is there no moral Spider within you to smooth it out, no patient will to weave a better web to-morrow than the one that was woven to-day? Perhaps to-morrow will tell, but before then you will have blessed the Spiders, and slowly made the confession that they were wonderfully wise old teachers when they gave you their web for a lesson.

CONSTANCE McKEAND.

Convent of Our Lady of the Sacred Heart, Oakland, Cal.

Courage

Courage ! faint heart, fear not the burden
   That is laid on your soul to-night ;
A comforting angel is near you
   Who will pity and make it seem light.

For with looks uplifted to Heaven,
   His home and yours too, you know,
He is asking the Master to strengthen
   The soul He is striking so low.

He hears the heart moan, and wonders
   That such should be thine to bear,
Ah ! the thought comes quickly after—
   His Son did a thorn-crown wear.

Then, never more seek to wander,
   Be cheerful in sunshine and rain,
Content that the Father looks on thee,
   To see if His child thou'lt remain.

Courage ! then, faint heart, never despair ;
   Courage ! and wait for the morrow,
When the dull clouds of care shall vanish away,
   Thou wilt wonder what was thy sorrow.—*Kate L. O'Neill.*

Bridal Veil Fall, Yosemite

I saw it when the moonlight kissed it
  With pensive beam and fair,
Weaving with bright noiseless fingers
  Diamonds in its flowing hair.
I saw it when the moonlight crowned it
  With a halo soft of light,
While its gentle voice sang softly
  Love songs to the peaceful night.
I heard its voice far in the distance
  Murmuring tenderly and sweet,
Echoing through the lonely mountains
  Like the tread of fairest feet.

Sweetest waters of the Valley!
  Is thy source far in the skies,
In some cloud that crowns some mountain
  Rising vast before mine eyes?
Ah! methinks the angels passing
  Drink beside thy limpid wave,
And from their bright lips thou stol'st
  Thy love songs tender and grave.
Ay! methinks their lips have taught thee
  The restful song thy sweet voice sings,
And thy glistening, fleecy whiteness,
  Thou didst steal from their white wings.

JOSEPHINE HALE.

Convent of Our Lady of the Sacred Heart, Oakland, Cal.

The First Snow-Fall

Down, down comes the light-footed snow, covering a green California landscape. Nearly fifteen years have I lived on the smiling Pacific Coast and never yet has the soft, feathery, dove-like snow visited us. It vests our trees and shrubs in a light glimmering mantle, and completely envelops the long cypress hedge in a pure valenciennes-lace, looped up here and there by a refractory twig that has protested against this new suit of white so strange yet so inexpressibly beautiful. It is an Eastern picture causing all our thoughts to fly to the home of our youth, and making our fingers tingle for a snow-ball frolic. Eastern I say, yet not so, because the jolly snow-elves have come on a surprise-party and instead of clothing bare branches, they try to hide the emerald perennial verdure that peeps out everywhere and laughs at them. The haughty evergreens and everlastings repel such liberties and rise out of the snow carpet. Here is a patch of lovely green grass softly kissed by the fleecy crystals.

And the flowers, oh! the sweet flowers! There I spy the red-hooded nasturtiums hiding, not under the smooth coverlet, but peeping out on the world at large. Here that creamy beauty, the tea-rose, inclines its head under the great load, and the sweet little buds that had mistaken winter for spring will not believe their eyes. In every direction the trailing vines shake out their long tendrils in the snowy air. The scarlet flowers of the passion-vine on the grotto of Our Lady, lay their cheeks on the white stones. How sweet the statue of the Virgin looks in her cloak of blue 'mid those immaculate surroundings. Every one exclaims: "Oh! I hope the snow will keep till to-morrow"! We are even afraid that some stray sun-beam will come and destroy our glimmering treasure. Alas! alas! it will soon disappear. I see it already losing its hold on the roofs where it lies so secure and smiling. The weather has commenced to drop tears over our disappointment. Thus with all our earthly joys—ever pleasing and ever-fleeting.

May the New Year bring us no deeper sorrow.

Oakland, Dec. 31, 1881.

Live not to Yourself Alone

※

Swaying in the soft gentle breath of morn, with the sunbeams glinting o'er its frail form, a blushing rose sang with the early choristers, sang in the voice of perfume : "I live not for myself alone, but even my little life has a loving mission to fulfill in God's great field of labor. I live to flood the atmosphere with my sweetest incense, and to speak and bring happiness to man's immortal soul. In the sunny tresses of the maiden I quietly nestle, and softly blush on the heaving bosom of the bride. Pale and silent I kiss the coffin-lid of the dead, or pleading at Our Lady's feet, I breathe a prayerful incense. Into my dewy depths the fairy humming-bird dips its dainty bill and darts on its gleaming way, refreshed with the nectar of my sweets. To the toiling bee I give the cloying honey with which he delights the taste of man. My odorous beauty breathes forth bright, gentle, holy thoughts, like a wreath of sunshine on life's troubled hours. Thus ever is my mission unselfish, thus ever do my delicate petals and dewy cup speak of God's goodness and beauty ;

and, whether born in the tender sunshine or in the sombre shadow, not for myself alone do I bud and blossom here, but to brighten this tear-dimmed earth.

High up on the bleak mountain-side, dim in the purple-blue distance, towers, lone and sad, an old oak-tree, waving its leafy banners to and fro. As it stands in the midst of desolation with nothing in this barren spot to which it can bring joy, something within you whispers that surely this tree lives to itself. " Not so," indignantly rustles the oak, " God never made me for a purpose so small. Four score and ten springs have smiled upon me, four score and ten summers have danced lightly o'er my boughs, while full as many autumns have touched my mantle with softest tints of crimson, gold and purple, and died into the bleakness of winter. Through all these years I have stood firm and undaunted, welcoming to my heart all who sought a refuge there, and into my arms each night I gathered the noisy birds and rocked them to sleep. In the still summer days when the sun casts its fevered rays upon the parched earth, the panting flocks fly to me and fall at my feet in the grateful shade which my waving branches cast upon them. In my bosom the soaring eagle builds his lonely nest, and when wintry storms shake me to my very roots, the proud bird rests secure in the shelter of my strong arms. In the dreamy summer-time the gauzy-winged butterfly flutters through the lace-work of my leaves and floats away again like a bright-colored blossom of the air. When the angry elements have united in war against each other, thunderbolts have burst at my feet, while my bosom has been seared and pierced by the lightning stroke which otherwise would have destroyed the weary traveller. The shrieking winds wrest from me my wealth of acorns and strew them over the earth. Years roll on, and what were once those tiny cups are now countless groves of trees which claim me as their parent. When God wills that I shall stand no longer, I shall fall by the hand of man and I will go to strengthen his ship which makes him lord of the ocean. And when the howling winds moan across the dreary moor, I will crackle upon the ample hearth and cast a ruddy glow upon the happy faces grouped around me. Now tell me, thoughtless one, if I live for myself."

Speak to the rushing streamlet that, blithe and boisterous dances adown the slanting hill. Now sparkling in the light, now sombre in the shadow, ever it bounds on heeding naught. But its merry voice rings out on the air, and as it bubbles over rock and pebble, kissing fern and blossom, its sweet song comes to me: "Mid snow-silvered precipices I found my icy course: but tired of my useless life so far above the earth, I broke my chilly fetters and in the quiet of midnight I plunged down the snow-mantled crags. Along my winding way I scatter life and health on every side. I ripple through the grassy meads and leave them gay with flowers. I meander through the pleasant valleys and sweeten the languid air in dreamy June, while from the rustling grasses that line my margin, the lark soars to greet the rising sun. I cheer the drooping summer flowers, refresh the thirsty cattle and weary birds, and sprinkle with modest daisies the golden corn fields. The sun loves me and draws me to him in waves of feathery vapor, and in the fresh spring days I float in great fleecy clouds through the blue expanse above. A chilly wind disturbs my garnered drops and lo! abrupt and loud I fall as glistening rain. I jewel the dainty blue-bell with my sparkling drops, and at sunrise, behold I have begemmed every blade of the lowly grass. Thus ever will I comfort man, and I will rise and fall, rise and fall till my loving mission is over."

Walk forth in the still calm night beneath the great dome of the sky; gaze upward upon that deep-blue expanse gleaming with color and brilliancy; see that distant star which beams tranquilly and softly upon you; whisper your question upon the midnight air, and the answer comes down the path of light: " Not for myself alone do I rise and set and sparkle in the diadem of the night. I have a wondrous work to perform—the holding together of a myriad of shining worlds. My rays beam alike on the great and the lowly, on the rich and the poor, bringing comfort to all. Many a time have I guided the poor lost sailor, from a hopeless realm of waters to his home and waiting mother. I am a mighty world supporting upon my bosom countless immortal beings worshipping the same Creator as you. Within my tiny zone I will ever linger, and with my bleak mountains and shadowy valleys, will ever sing my part in the harmony of the spheres. I do not merely gem the sky, but my far-off lights are a constant reminder to man of his heavenly home which waits ever ready for his coming. Upon the jetty coronet of night I write in letters of gold the power and goodness, and majesty, of Him, who formed me and my myriad sisters, for the service of man."

For Him was created every little flower that blows, every breeze that carries its sweet burden of incense over the earth, every tendril of the clinging vine, every dewdrop glistening in the blue-bell cup: and the lesson they teach is one of unselfishness and duty.

Ah! man, "thou who art earth's honored priest," thou the chief guest at love's ungrudging feast of beauty, canst thou live blindly to thyself alone? Spurn self, put it aside, and live only to God and thy neighbor.

NELLIE WHITE,   ZOE CHADWICK.

Convent of Our Lady of the Sacred Heart, Oakland, Cal.

The Gift of a Smile

❊

Have you ever known what it was to feel the influence of a smile? Surely you have ; and not knowing the workings of your young, tender heart, could not guess exactly what it was that gave such happiness. Yes ; smiles are truly as the breath of heaven, when given to some sorrow or care-worn heart. In school, dear children, has not your teacher's smile of approval sent a thrill through your soul more precious than all rewards, and have you not gone home with a heart full of content and peaceful joy? Let me tell you a little incident of recent occurrence. Death had touched the brow of a young girl of some thirteen years. Into the crowded room where the dead child lay, came a girl of about the same age; her face bore the look of those who carry sorrow even in the heart of their youth. She handed a little bouquet to one present, saying, "I am sorry I could not give her more; although we never spoke, yet she always smiled at me so kindly that I brought her this; I am so sorry she is dead;" and left as quietly as she entered. If you could know how much this "gift of a smile" cheers a heart, you would be more generous with your smiles, particularly to the poor and unfortunate. Let not riches buy your smiles, but remember Jesus smiled on the unfortunate. You do it in His imitation.

MARY J. DOLAN.

Convent of the Holy Names, San Francisco, Cal.

The Lost Chord

Somewhere in the vast expanse between heaven's blue and the chaos of earth, there is a chord trembling and lone; it is in vain we search for it, we hear the faint tones murmuring through the long crystal corridors of space, but it is only an echo, and then the melody is gone. The great harp of the universe, whose strings were once tuned in perfect harmony, now gives forth only unfinished melodies, since the rude hand of Sin broke the chord of obedience to the Creator; but far away in remote space, that one lost chord ever faintly murmurs its repinings for its golden sister strings.

Every day, and in every stage of life, from the rosy-tinted
dawn of childhood, to the heavy-clouded mid-day of manhood,
and still farther on to the days colored by the last mellow rays of
the setting sun of life, poor mortals search in vain for this lost
chord which would render complete the harmony of their life. In
infancy, the soul's young harp, twined with Purity's fairest flowers,
vibrates with the music of innocence, but some careless hand
snaps one of the delicate strings, and, alas! the harmony is broken
and the chord is lost. Yet despair not, fair child, some day when
the harp of life is silent, back from its mystic wanderings will
come that absent string and the soul will vibrate with heavenly
music.

In the happy circle that lingers round the fireside, we miss a
tone from the sweet song of happiness, one tone which is wanting to
complete the rich harmony. The vacant chair murmurs in sad,
minor notes of one who has crossed over the silver bridge which
spans the dark waters of Eternity, to the heavenly shore from
which, through the azure corridor lighted by the glittering gems,
comes the faint echo of the missing chord. It is in vain we try to
catch it, it is gone like the shadow of an angel's wing, and we only
know that some day our harp will be completed.

Later on we meet a seeker for the missing link to the chain of
harmony, in the silver-haired man, whose harp is now bathed in
the rays of light from the heavenly shore, as his bark gently glides
down the ebbing stream, but from among its golden strings one is
missing. Soon, ah! soon, will angel hands replace the missing
chord, and tune again the soul's rich harp to breathe newer, rarer,
sweeter tones.

Sometimes when from the dusky hand of night, the shadows of
Twilight are softly falling, and the heart's secret cares and sorrows·
are wooed to rest by the mystic voice of Peace, as the blossoms are
caressed into slumber by the evening breeze and all Nature seems in
one sweet dream, strains of music greet our ear, and our spirit
soars away on Fancy's wing to seek the lost string which breaks the

CORRIDOR

LIBRARY

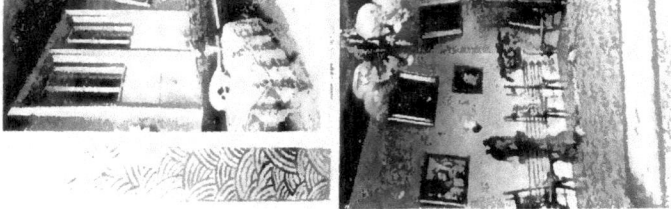

MUSIC HALL   PARLORS

CONVENT OF OUR LADY OF THE SACRED HEART, OAKLAND, CAL.

harmony. In rapturous dreams we find seraphic beings, bearing from the realms of bliss the missing chord ; but it is only a phantasy, and we wake to find, as before, the soul's secret harp murmuring for the missing link of harmony.

How beautiful is the idea of the "Music of the Spheres!" Imagine each of the gems that appear as mere glittering points, giving forth melody of divinest nature, and all blending in harmony. That is a concert fit only for the pure ears of angels, it is far too heavenly for the gross ear of man. Yet here too, one tone of harmony is gone, for the rude touch of Sin on our earth has broken the chord which should render perfect the music, and not till it be restored by the all-powerful, all-merciful hand of God, will the melody, which now sinks of its own heaviness, rise through the azure curtain in purest praises to the Eternal Throne.

Some day when all earth's weary wanderers shall stand with their broken harps on the brink of Eternity, they will see gleaming through the opening portals, the lost chord which has rendered the harmony of their lives incomplete, and when the past years float like a dreamy panorama before their eyes, they will then know that

> "It may be that Death's bright angel,
>   Will speak in that chord again,
> It may be that only in Heaven,
>   They shall hear that grand AMEN!"

> —A. Proctor.

FANNIE CARROLL.

Convent of Our Lady of the Sacred Heart, Oakland, Cal.

Lines on a Feast Day

*

A time-stained volume, quaint and old,
    And musingly I turn it o'er,
Perchance those pages dark with mold,
    Strange stories tell of days of yore—
Are gemmed with words and thoughts of gold.

Vain is the hope ; all interest lost,
    The gray leaves flutter to and fro ;
But ah ! a perfume rare is tost,
    That scents those dismal pages so—
A faded bloom with memories fraught.

So in the volume of the year,
    There hidden lies a fragrant rose :
Over the gloomy days, and drear,
    The sweetest of incense it throws—
"A day of days " to us so dear.

Our cherished teacher's feast day fair,
    Rich with fond memories of the past,
Of tender words, and loving care,
    Of golden hours too bright to last
O vanished days, so sweet and rare!

Annie Carey.

Convent of the Holy Names, San Francisco, Cal.

The Shell was not filled with Pearls until it was contented.

(i.e. ceased from unrest)

Persian

✳

Look upon the sea at the dawn of a summer's day. The pale blue waves, tipped by the rosy hues of the morning light, are singing their hymns of praise in tones of sweetest music. The golden beach is their altar, it is here they come to sing and pray, and then go back into the sea to come again and go once more, for, to and fro, has Heaven marked the pathway of the waves on the avenues of time. And when the sun has set, and the sable shadows have fallen, and myriads of stars are crowning the brow of night, behold those children of the deep, clad in dark blue garments and decked with the jewels that Heaven has lent them, and listen to their glorious chant. How sublime! how seemingly unearthly! can it be the echo's own refrain of the immortal Te Deum of Paradise?

O beautiful waves upon a summer sea! ye are the image of sinless hearts singing in grateful accents at the Feet of God the prelude of everlasting life.

But the sea is not always tranquil, for it is a mirror of all men's hearts, and these differ as the vicissitudes of light and shade.

Watch the birds with snowy wings flying westward over the waves into the evening sun. In the east hear the muffled sounds of the tempest's roar. Suddenly the sky grows dark and great winds come. Huge billows rise and dash angrily against the cliffs in cries of wildest agony. It is the fury of a storm. It is the picture of another storm upon the ocean of life, when the winds of passion arise. There are hearts which like the birds fly unto the Light when the threatening sounds are heard afar, but alas! there are others, impetuous as the waves, that strike against the rocks of despair, and fall like their foam into the sea.

Let us leave the surface of the deep and descend, where the tumult of winds and waves is all unheard, into that mysterious region where perpetual silence reigns, and where untold beauty lives unseen by human eye. There in some fair garden or in some jeweled cave lies a shell filled with pearls of rarest lustre. It is the book in which God has sweetly written the simile of a faithful heart's life and recompense. He breathed the parable into the ear of some Persian poet who wrote it thus in his book of meditations: " The shell was not filled with pearls until it was contented." It pictures the home of a tiny life whose vital spark is now extinguished. It tells its years of continuous labor and of patient endurance, gathering grains of sand and intruding fragments, perhaps of rock or of some other shell, which caused it pain, and how it ceased not from unrest, until of each it had formed a pearl of purest splendor.

O happy the hearts that on life's great ocean gather golden deeds, afflictions and sorrows! In a few short years when the work is accomplished, what joy when God shall open the shell and find it filled with pearls; these alone are the earthly treasures that can purchase immortality.

ELIZA OVIEDO.

Convent of the Holy Names, San Francisco, Cal.

Farewell to April and Welcome to May

✛

Farewell! wayward, laughing April, month of smiles and tears. We had grown to love you, when you ceased to be; and did you not love us, too? Yes; for when May was ushered in in all the dreamy newness of life, tears of regret, I ween, at leaving us, still lingered, sparkling like so many diamonds on the flowers. But while we say, "Vale, dear April," we would thank you for the many joys and pleasures you brought us; and, although other months may bring us like happiness, like joys, like pleasures, still yours will ever smile with softer glow; around them ever shall circle a halo of wondrous beauty, studded with rarest gems—the halo, a sunny smile, the gems, sparkling tears. What crown more bright! what gems, what jewels more precious?

Will our hearts thus eulogize you, sweet May, when your course is run? Oh! yes; for what heart that loves our Blessed Mother, can fail to love her month? What poet has not sung the praises of this month, and of her whose name it bears? What a month of song, of pleasures and of smiles! What a joyous time for heart and soul! How happy, how light-hearted we feel as we wander through the meadows and fields of clover, or climb the hills and from each sunny slope cull the brightest, fairest flowers! How our souls rejoice, when, in the sweet even-tide, we gather round her altars, and sing the hymns of praise and love to our Mother!

Charming May! Each year we welcome her just as heartily, even though the rose color of our lives be blanched to snowy whiteness, and a shaft of marble records a grave in the cemetery of our souls. Sweet herald of approaching summer, we hail you! We welcome you with your birds, your flowers, your soft winds. Your birds we shall teach to carol the praise of our Queen; your choicest flowers we shall lay at her feet; and your winds—sweet with much kissing of the roses, shall waft fragrance to her throne above.

Oh, how happy we shall be, if, when death's cold lips have touched ours, whether it be in the May of lives, or in sullen, dark November, we shall go straight to Mary's feet, there to sit and listen to her gentle voice, as she tells us how much she has ever loved us; how much she has longed to have her children near her. Oh, happiness untold—thus to be with Mary! Oh, quick, the hour that will cut the moorings of our life-bark and set it adrift on the home-going tide.

Nora Fitzgerald.

Convent of the Holy Names, San Francisco, Cal.

Shakespeare

Many an age has been prolific of great minds and lofty geniuses, but the age of Elizabeth surpasses them all, not only in the number and variety of the master-minds of that period, but especially in this:—that it included within its charmed circle, the greatest genius of his time, and it may be of all time. For of all the stars in that bright galaxy which clustered round the throne of Elizabeth, Shakespeare shines resplendent and solitary.

Ages had come and gone, before Shakespeare was, and ages have passed since Shakespeare has been, yet, not one has produced a single spirit, so lofty in genius or so transcendent in glory. Not one is there fit even to touch the hem of the peculiar robe, with which he has clothed himself in his immortal conceptions, and by which we, at all times recognize our own Shakespeare: namely: his power of depicting human life and human affairs and all their accompanying cares, passions and fancies.

Some poets, as Milton and Dante have taken grand and awful themes for their songs. They ascend into the very heavens and describe the scenes thereof; they hold converse with both angels and demons. But there is a limit. Their genius exhausts itself, and when they would approach the earth, they stumble and totter as though they did not know their way amid such lowness.

Others "of the earth, earthly" have not the wings wherewith to soar to higher spheres, and nobler climes. They find in the goodness and beauty of earth, something of that greater beauty which attracts their brother spirits and which floating, like a seraph, twixt heaven and earth, whilst it eludes, still leads them on. For poesy though a captive here below has its true home above, and in the hearts where it makes its abode, it must ever create that longing for the higher beauty beyond. Ah! far beyond the conception of those "lesser lights," but which leaves them ever watching and waiting and striving to catch the "lost chords" of the heavenly alleluias, amid the lowness of earth.

With Shakespeare it was different, nothing was so high that he could not reach; nothing so low that he could not fathom, nothing so subtle that he could not grasp; nothing so grand that he could not comprehend; nothing so beautiful that he could not portray, and nothing so complex, that he could not divide and make clear and commingle again into one gorgeous whole, and drape and fashion it with the diverse fancies and creations of his fertile brain, until naught was left untried that could be done, and naught was left unsaid, that could be sung.

Nothing daunted, nothing repelled him. He handled spirits and mortals with the same vigorous grasp, and they danced or moped in mirth or melancholy, obedient to his powerful will, portrayed with such consummate art as to have made the world look on in amazement and wonder for more than three hundred years.

Hideous witches, wrapt in air, taunt and prophesy; spectral forms appear to affright, and instruct unto vengeance and death; heart-withering visions with their dire signs appear, to torment or predict, whilst fairies gambol and revel to their hearts' content in sunlit glade or moon-tipped grove.

But it is especially in depicting all that pertains to man and humanity that shows forth Shakespeare's greatest powers. He becomes as it were, each of his different characters in turn. He is at once the parricide, the jealous husband, the trustful woman, the conspirator, the spy, the fickle prince, the crafty statesman, the faithful friend, the noble lord, the mindful servant, the supercilious knave. They pass before our minds in ever lengthening procession; and Shakespeare stands guard over all, for was it not his immortal pen which has called them all into being? Truly is he great in their greatness. Once known we associate with their vice or their virtue, the vices and virtues of their kind.

Wolsey and Macbeth are synonyms of ambition; Othello and Iago, of jealousy and deceit; Portia, of prudence, discretion, and generous love; Bassanio and Antonia, of faithful, noble friendship; Hamlet, of indifference and indecision; Ophelia of despairing love. Shylock and his merciless greed of gold, Brutus and his ingratitude, Katherine and her untamed anger and Cordelia of dauntless truth and noble mind, these are names, which are blended so thoroughly with the aims and passions of the characters represented that it is impossible to separate the one from the other. They serve as landmarks, as it were, showing forth the forms of that greater beauty, to be found only as the whole grand vista unfolds before us, with all its diverse scenery, and all its glorious hues and images. Each step discloses new beauties, until, almost inebriated, we stand and survey the whole, and with all the fires of enthusiasm kindled within us, we must needs cry "enough!"

One is overwhelmed when contemplating that grand mental power, which reflects, as in a mirror, the manifold passions and emotions, the heartfelt joys and sorrows of the human heart, for all

ST. ROSE'S SCHOOL, S. E.

CHILDREN OF MARY'S SODALITY HALL,
CONVENT OF THE HOLY NAMES

CONVENT OF THE HOLY NAMES, ST. JOSEPH'S PARISH, S. E.

CHAPEL, CONVENT OF THE HOLY NAMES

time is enshrined in these immortal plays, which have served to lift their creator to the very skies, above all other men and leave him there in solitary, unique, delightful grandeur.

KATE L. O'NEILL.

Convent of the Holy Names, San Francisco, Cal.

Carmelo

The quaint old town of Monterey contains many objects of interest for the student of the past. There, on the golden shores of the Pacific, are ruins that speak eloquently of devoted zeal and charity—relics of a departed race—among them, the old structure known as Carmel Mission. Around each crumbling wall cling memories of the days when the good Padres struggled and toiled in enduring patience, conquering with the cross, long before General Fremont raised the American flag on the heights of Monterey.

A pleasant, yet mournful feeling is aroused when gazing upon a ruin; lessons on the mutability of earthly things, the littleness of man, come to us as we observe that every effort to make himself immortal only mocks him, telling forcibly of his passing existence.

When we gaze on the Missions, thoughts of the great, the good, the noble awaken within us, and when we see these relics of love and tireless zeal shattered, our admiration is more deeply excited.

The Missions of California stand in humble silence as monuments of the devotedness of the beloved Padres. They are found along the coast from San Diego's shore to San Rafael's forest; their fallen walls and crumbling towers speaking pathetically of days that are no more.

11

Carmel Mission was erected in 1770 by Junipero Serra; it is situated in the fertile Carmel Valley, a short distance from the bay of the same name, and about five miles from the historic town of Monterey. The Mission is built of sandstone and concrete; the roof was originally made of tiles, but is now replaced by one of shingles. The structure was raised by the Indians under the guidance of the Fathers, and shows signs of skilled workmanship combined with patient toil. Before reaching the Mission one passes through grainfields and orchards put under cultivation by the Padres, thus showing that they did not neglect to till the land in their efforts to convert the heathen.

The ruins of adobe buildings once occupied by the Indians, are to the front of the church. The church itself faces the northeast, and on approaching, one sees the arched facade on either side of which rise towers, the larger one surmounted by a dome. In this campanile hung the silver-tongued bells of the Mission, which for years pealed so sweetly, proclaiming peace and good will to the Indian. Above the entrance is a star-shaped window; in the belfry are three windows, two facing the north, one the east.

For many years the building was crumbling rapidly to decay, and relic hunters took away tiles, portions of woodwork, in fact, anything they could secure. Father Cassanova, Pastor of Monterey, was grieved to think Padre Serra's work was being so despoiled; for years he had his heart set on preserving the last resting place of this venerable priest and his co-laborers. Thanks to his zeal, it is now partially restored to its former condition.

Once inside the church a deep reverence fills the visitor; we are carried back to the past; the church seems filled with its swarthy worshippers, and we almost hear the choir chanting its weird vesper hymn. There is the same pulpit from which Father Serra preached to his flock; some of the stained glass windows, representing Christ and the Blessed Virgin, also remain; the wooden altar is now replaced by one of marble; near by is a small slab with the inscription: "Fundata A. D. 1770; Restorata 1884." Sleeping near the altar with his fellow laborers lies Junipero Serra. Resting there is he who in life guided his children so well, and in death still seems to watch over his faithful Indians, who sleep in a neighboring cemetery.

The Indians have a beautiful legend which tells how on Christmas of every year Padre Serra rises from his tomb and celebrates midnight mass.

The only ornaments left in the church are an old plaster statue of the Blessed Virgin, about a foot in height, a few old paintings of our Lord and the saints. To the left of the church is the baptistry, which contained the baptismal font, now restored. On the walls of the baptistry was a prayer once recited by the Indians, but it has been so defaced by relic hunters that its meaning can scarcely be ascertained. Some kind lady has had the words re-written and framed. Among the other relics are the records of the church in Serra's own handwriting; a rich and rare old Bible bearing the date 1589, which was used by the Padres; Serra's confessional, a splendidly carved piece of work; a painting of St. Rose of Lima, and other paintings, are still in a good state of preservation, and are to be seen in San Carlos' Church in the town of Monterey. They were taken there before Carmel was restored, as it was not deemed safe to leave anything of value within its tottering walls.

Thus are scattered the mementos of the happy days that are gone forever, but none can touch the wooded hills, no human finger limit the boundless sea. As in the days of the "black-robes," the "murmuring pines" still sing responsive to the dirge of the ocean—a requiem chant they ever, while the slumbering land awaits a new resurrection to the busy scenes of yore.

NELLIE FEEHAN.

Convent of the Holy Names, San Francisco, Cal.

School-Day Memories

✳

A well-known author has written ; " to call up our old days shall be a solemn pleasure yet," and the words can hardly be more fitly applied than to looking backward on our school life, overflowing as it is with tender memories and useful lessons ; lessons that were learned for Time, and lessons bearing fruit for Eternity.

Years have gone by, and the mist of time has gathered between the present and the past, but even as the last rays of the setting sun fall athwart our path, and seem all the brighter for the dim evening light, and before the twilight shadows creep about us, so the recollections of our school-days come to us now with a more tender and grateful affection, when we have borne for awhile the burden and heat of the day, in our life in the world ; the life that looked bright and fair when we knew it but in our dreams, and the reality of which has been a stern awakening to many.

What changes have taken place in these few years! How many breaks in the little circle to which we look back, and call fondly " Our Class" or " the girls in our room."

The Angel of Death has entered and breathed on the fairest flowers. The Angels of Love and of Prayer have whispered to others calling them to a nobler and a higher life. And the Angel of Duty stands by the rest, pointing with unerring finger to the path that ends in peace ; now leading us gaily onward in the joyous freedom of children doing their Father's will, now gently chiding when our footsteps are too hasty or too slow, and ever and anon, pausing before us and with sterner mien, demanding some hardly wrought sacrifice.

And in the highest Heaven of the favored few, in the seclusion of the Cloister, as well as in the walks and avenues of our daily life, the Convent lessons bear their fruit. For some, a glorious reward : for others, the peace of lives " hidden with Christ in God;" and for us, who will say that in the hourly struggle with the world without us, and the world within, the lessons of our earlier years do not give strength to our weak hearts, inspire us with higher motives and nobler aspirations, and so lead us ever onward and upward.

Tenderly we look backward, and beg a blessing on the generous souls who have left all at the voice of Heaven, and devote their lives to enlightening the minds, and guiding the hearts of children.

Softly we breathe a prayer for those who have gone before, and bow our heads in humble submission to the Providence of God.

And for ourselves we plead, oh, so fervently! for grace to be faithful to the teaching of by-gone days, that the tiny seeds sown long ago, growing and flourishing with time, may at length put forth flowers that will bloom in the Divine Garden, and exhale forever the perfume of virtues taught us in our days of innocence and childhood faith.

LAURA J. BRENHAM.

Convent of the Holy Names, San Francisco, Cal.

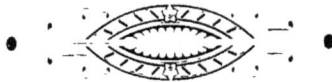

Within a Soul

❖

Man has an unquenchable thirst for the unknown. Since Eve listened to the voice of the Tempter—' ye shall be like Gods'—the curiosity which prompted her to know what she should have ignored, descended as a legacy to the human race.

The Unknown—what a promise for the cravings of the mind, anxious to hoard up new stores of knowledge, and what obstacles will arrest man on his unexplored pathway? Is it appalling danger? Is it heat or cold, misery or famine, disease or death that cause him to tarry in his eager pursuit? . . . See him searching into the bowels of the earth, turning up the dust of ages, ascending the current of Time, clasping hands as it were with his prehistoric brethren—deciphering barbaric symbols until the Past almost ceases to be. A quarter of a century ago vast unexplored areas covered our maps—these hidden and almost inaccessible regions have echoed and re-echoed the civilized voice, and the veil is rent, behind which was sequestered the great Unknown. From Polar regions to Africa's burning sands and Antarctic snows, man has left his trace, and ofttimes his bleaching bones tell us, both of his struggles and his failures in his persistent research. Into the realms of space Science has led him until the orbs above have been brought into close proximity with the ever-searching mind of man, and there seems little left to surmise. This active, seething, craving spirit has anticipated ages ahead, and to-day we find ourselves face to face with such a state of progress that the mental stature of the 19th Century will be comparatively lilliputian to the enlightened races of the future.

Is there any hidden recess left which man's restless mind has not penetrated? any stronghold which he has not taken by storm? Ah, yes! there is a world around us, which the keenest eye fails to penetrate—a realm so subtle, so spiritual, so guarded from all encroachments, save the all-seeing eye of God, that we hardly divine its existence.

We live with bodies, see the actions of men, listen to their speech, but can we safely affirm that all these manifestations are but so many reflections of the spirit within?

There are natures so constituted, that through their transparency are revealed the workings of the soul. Yet, even these have their own inner sanctuary in which God walks alone, as with our first parents before the fall.

Others are clogged by the body, as by an iceberg ; the fire within burns fiercely, but like the pent-up volcano, finds no issue. The

reticent man, shut up within himself, bows under the humiliating verdict of being soulless, when the very fact of his having so much soul, makes him the most unfortunate of beings.

The wary and deceitful plays his part so skillfully that no suspicion rests upon his base motives, so secure is he behind the barrier of the senses—and what marvel at this security? since it has been his life-long study to make this barrier impenetrable to the eye of his fellow-beings.

Indeed, so subtle are the workings of the spirit within, that the most honest and upright are often at a loss to account for the intentions which underlie their seemingly best deeds.

Some there are, again, who abhor publicity, and make to themselves a dwelling apart ; so isolated are their lives, that only a restricted circle of friends are admitted to their intimacy, and even these are excluded from the inner chamber, into which no human eye is permitted to intrude.

"God breathed into man the breath of life"—this is His own Image. No human effort can reproduce it, no power annihilate it, no eye search into the depths thereof, save the Creator Himself.

True, Science as with all unknown truths, gives principles, by which the faculties of this spiritual part of our being are analyzed; but how much is left unexplored! Let us take an individual soul—'tis a world by itself, in which the passions, sensibilities and emotions are playing the most wondrous drama that was ever enacted. It is also a battlefield, upon which the man of flesh and the man of spirit are contending for the mastery. Each has its champions, and little do we know of the fierce contest, otherwise we would be less hasty in bestowing blame, more merciful and forgiving—yea, little do we know of the onslaught of the foe—of the long and weary resistance, of the bitterness of defeat. The battlefield is a bloodless one, but forth from the arena, come body and soul, gray with the struggle.

Turning from so painful a prospect, let us fix our eyes upon a more consoling one. We would see the soul, with God-like aspirations, cherishing the good, the beautiful and the true—victorious over the ignoble passions, growing in wisdom and godliness. Ah! this is a temple in which God finds His delight ! The Saints and the Just have told us their experience, in these regions away from the haunts of worldliness and sin ; but with eyes of flesh, we are blind to such spiritual beauties, and it will be given to us only in the glories of the Resurrection, to conceive the greatness of this immortal spirit, and its capabilities of assimilating itself with the Almighty Being that brought it into existence. The Spouse in the Canticle calls the soul of His beloved, a sealed garden, in which bloom myrrh, spikenard and all precious ointments. All the glory, the beauty, and the fragrance of the world of flowers can give us no idea of this garden of the Spouse ; of its loveliness, its variety, its inebriating fragrance. The world catches but faint glimpses of what the saints have told of themselves. The Spouse has His hidden recesses, which are veiled to mortal eyes, His own secrets with His beloved. For the beauty of the daughter of Sion is all interior, saith the inspired volume. Therefore, we know little of souls, and of the Holy Spirit's operations therein.

Beginning at the lowest degree of human life, and ascending the scale gradually, we marvel at the workings of Divine Grace— in the babe merging from the baptismal waters ; in the predestined child, who has escaped all contaminating influence, and the purity of whose soul makes it less a thing of earth than of Heaven ; in youth, and at a maturer period, as well as down the slope of years, we see the faithful observer of God's law on his silent round of duty garnering in a golden harvest, of which human statistics take no account, until this grand tableau culminates in the hoary-headed sire, standing in the glow of the Eternal Summits, yearning daily for the final merging of his soul into the bosom of that Being Who created him. Ah! if we lived in this world of souls, how much more beauty we would discover in our surroundings, how much more hallowed the ground upon which we tread!

Touching upon these souls as it were at every turning point, should it not strike awe into our hearts, knowing all the wonders that God is working therein? Physical defects which give birth to petty dislikes and repugnances, would disappear in the overwhelming moral greatness of these godlike spirits—for, says a noted writer, "It is the soul shining through the face that makes one beautiful."

What a panorama will be unveiled to our gaze on the great day of the revelation of souls! and, like the disciples 'mid the unexpected glories of Thabor, we will then have no aspirations beyond that Tabernacle where God and His dearly bought souls have met, in an everlasting embrace of love and peace.

Therefore let us love souls, live with souls, study souls; it will make our lives better, purer, holier, "until this corruption puts on incorruption, and this mortal puts on immortality."

A LOVER OF SOULS.

Then and Now

※

The years have passed, and flown apace,
   As summer birds do fly,
That cast their shadows as they flit
   O'er earth and field and sky.

Those shadows which must turn to gold
   When veined by heaven's rays,
If good and noble deeds are wrought
   Within the fleeting days.

*   *   *   *   *

Now, Mem'ry lift on high thy rod
  As Moses did of old ;
And bid the waves of Time roll back
  And show thy strand, unmarked, unscrolled.

*   *   *   *   *

Canadian shores gleam fair and bright,
  And Nature smiles on all,
When from the far-off western world,
  Sounds forth a bugle call.

A call to duty! Rise and come,
  Ye daughters of the King!
He calls to ye, and shall ye wait
  Or from ye nobly fling

All thoughts of self, of home and friends,
  Who only know His Will?
Ah! five and twenty years have passed,
  And yet they serve Him still!

Gaily as bride unto the feast
  Where love doth shine on all,
Go forth that band from Canada's shores,
  To hearken to the call.

Courage and strength and faith had they,
  Those chosen of the Lord.
And conquerors they stand to-day,
  Who preached not by the sword.

But by the kind and loving care
  They gave to all who came,
For knowledge, consolation, love,
  And asked in Jesus' Name.

For by that Name, before whose might
  Earth, heaven and hell must fall,
And by sweet Mary's tender Name,
  Have they accomplished all.

And that small band, led on by one
  Well formed by grace to guide,
Has grown and flourished day by day,
  Its works show far and wide.

A structure grand on high is reared,
  And lifts to heaven its dome,
As if to show the careless eye,
  That *there* above is *Home*.

Religion, Science, Art here meet,
  And flourish 'neath the care,
Of those who many years ago,
  First sowed the seedlings there.

And now the bearded grain is ripe,
  And she who sowed so true,
Has come to gather in the sheaves,
  And take *in love* her due.

Then side by side, and heart to heart,
  We welcome her in glee,
Our souls glad hallelujahs sing
  In love's mute minstrelsy.

And while we send on high our voice,
  On high too speeds the pray'r,
That God our Mother's heart will fill,
  With sweetest love *fore'er*.

And he whose voice sent forth the call
  Which reached the distant land,
Has Father, Brother, friend long been,
  To his devoted band.

Ah! come, sweet Peace, and crown his days,
  Who all his days has spent,
In "strivings oft, in perils deep;"
  And hope and courage lent,

To all who claimed a Father's care ;
 And none e'er asked for aught,
But it was given in joy. Ah! come
 Sweet Peace—the crown is sought.

And our own Mother, whom God has given
 Sweet womanhood's true grace,
Whose mother soul doth bend to all,
 Who well doth fill her place,

In truest worth, in guidings wise,
 Whose rule is love's own sway :
Ah! long may she be ours to love
 Long may she point the way

To higher things, and nobler far,
 Than this world e'er controls ;
So may our lives meet here through God,
 In God, above, our souls.

*   *   *   *   *

Now, Time, who in thy flowing tide,
 Dost bear all onward still,
Let not the Future mar the Past,
 But fairer, brighter still,

Ah! may the round of Duty, wrought
 In faith and hope and love,
A guerdon fair on earth e'er be
 A fadeless crown above.

KATE L. O'NEILL.

L' Envoi.

"To have ideas is to gather flowers, to think is to weave them into a [wreath]
Behold these fragrant blossoms culled from the [garden?]
of many a soul, woven into chaplets by loving h[ands]
and laid by loyal children at the feet of their Alma [Mater]

During the past twenty five years, a varying [number?]
of souls have wandered through the halls of the Convent[.]
Some, the loving Father has looked upon kindly, and ga[thered]
[ne]arly to His Sacred Heart. These too, would we remembe[r]
with bright smile and tender greeting, we meet each othe[r]
for the absent, a wreath of immortelles, for us, a crown of me[mory]
For some, the summer clouds have floated serenely, tinted wi[th]
hue of Nature's brush; to others, the days have been often da[rk and]
cloud covered. But, in the midst of them all, spread out in [the]
hazy past, lies the long stretch of happy school days, the [?]
of these days growing stronger, more salient as the years [pass]
on, silvering the golden tresses, and furrowing the snowy [brow]

Go then, little volume, Speak to the dear ones; tell them of the [?]
raised within the souls of their children, where virtue and virtuous [deeds?]
live, and perpetuate the good seed sown from generation unto gene[ration]
even on to the golden years that will encircle our Alma Mater [with]
an aureole significant of the eternal Years of Glory.

THIS BOOK IS DUE ON THE LAST DATE
STAMPED BELOW

AN INITIAL FINE OF 25 CENTS
WILL BE ASSESSED FOR FAILURE TO RETURN
THIS BOOK ON THE DATE DUE. THE PENALTY
WILL INCREASE TO 50 CENTS ON THE FOURTH
DAY AND TO $1.00 ON THE SEVENTH DAY
OVERDUE.

APR 25 1941